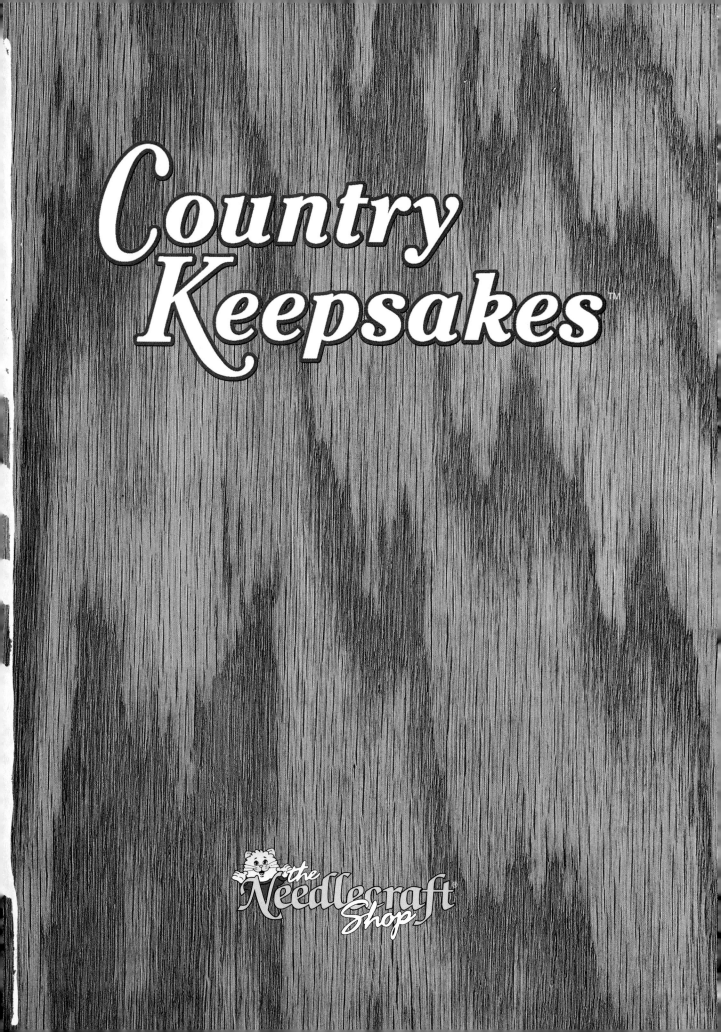

Country Keepsakes™

the Needlecraft® Shop

Interim Editorial Director: *Janet Tipton Perrin*
Product Development Manager: *Fran Rohus*
Production/Photography Director: *Ange Van Arman*

Editorial
Senior Editor: *Nancy Harris*
Editor: *Kris Kirst*
Editorial Team: *Jeanne Austin, Judy Crow,*
Jaimie Davenport, Shirley Patrick
Product Presentation Copy: *Jennifer McClain*
Copy Editor: *Salway Sabri*

Production
Book & Cover Design: *Clayton Lothrop*
Production Manager/Color Specialist: *Betty Holmes*
Production Coordinator: *Glenda Chamberlain*

Photography
Photography Manager: *Scott Campbell*
Photographers: *Keith Godfrey, Andy J. Burnfield*
Photo Stylist: *Martha Coquat*

Product Design
Design Coordinator: *Tonya Flynn*
Publications Coordinator: *Janet Birch*

Business
C.E.O: *John Robinson*
Vice President/Marketing: *Greg Deily*

Credits
Sincerest thanks to all the designers, manufacturers and other professionals
whose dedication has made this book possible. Special thanks to
Quebecor Printing Book Group, Kingsport, TN.
Copyright © 1999 The Needlecraft Shop, LLC

Library of Congress Cataloging-in-Publication Data
ISBN: 1-57367-110-X
First Printing: 1999
Library of Congress Catalog Card Number: 99-75970
Published and Distributed by
The Needlecraft Shop, LLC, Big Sandy, Texas 75755
Printed in the United States of America.

Dear Friends,

Everyone has something that is precious to him or her. Some small token of sentiment acquired at a special moment, from a special person. My most treasured tokens are those handmade by someone I love, like hand-colored pictures, a selected collage of photographs or a hand-stitched item. The time and creativity that went into each item sends the message to me that I am appreciated and loved. When I need an extra little pick-me-up, I admire these handmade treasures and visualize the time and effort someone spent just for me.

Country Keepsakes is full of special sentiments that can be stitched for someone you love, whether it is yourself, a friend, or family member. The variety of projects is sure to suit someone special on your "I'm thinking of you" list. And to help others appreciate the love of handmade gifts, we've also included a section of quick-to-stitch projects you can make for a local craft sale.

Share the love of needlework and tell someone they are extra special when you stitch something from this specially selected collection of keepsakes, Country Keepsakes.

Jan

~*Table of Contents*~

 **Old World Charm**

 **Farm Friends**

 **Garden Sunshine**

Hearts & Lace

'Tis the Season

Quick & Easy Bazaar

Old World Charm

Capture the beauty of days gone-by
with this treasure chest of treats to
stitch. Vintage style is at your fingertips
in this splendid old-fashioned collection,
just waiting to be brought to life. Create
holiday designs and hostess gifts to
compliment any décor, or make handy
helpers with homespun charm to fill your
days with ease. With this classic assortment,
you can stitch a rich tapestry of designs
for year-round pleasure to lend simple
elegance to every room. From bed to bath,
from kitchen to hearth, you'll enjoy the
memories evoked by patterns of quilts,
apples, cherubs and more - fashioned into
projects with lasting appeal.

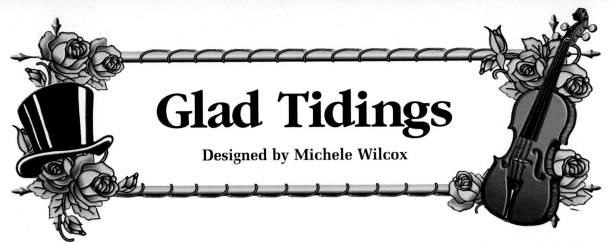

Glad Tidings

Designed by Michele Wilcox

SIZE
7½" x 11½" [19.1cm x 29.2cm].

SKILL LEVEL: Easy

MATERIALS
- ❑ One sheet of 7-count plastic canvas
- ❑ #5 pearl cotton or six-strand embroidery floss; for amount see Color Key.
- ❑ Worsted-weight or plastic canvas yarn; for amounts see Color Key.

CUTTING INSTRUCTIONS
For Lantern Motif, cut one according to graph.

STITCHING INSTRUCTIONS
1: Using colors indicated and Continental Stitch, work according to graph. With matching colors as shown in photo, Overcast edges.

2: Using pearl cotton or three strands floss and embroidery stitches indicated, embroider detail as indicated on graph.

3: Hang or display as desired.✽

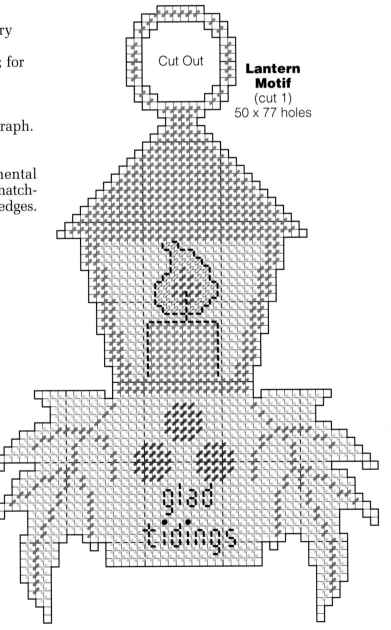

Cut Out

Lantern Motif
(cut 1)
50 x 77 holes

COLOR KEY: Glad Tidings

#5 pearl cotton			AMOUNT
■ Black			4 yds. [3.7m]

Worsted-weight	Nylon Plus™	Need-loft®	YARN AMOUNT
▨ Eggshell	#24	#39	16 yds. [14.6m]
▨ Black	#02	#00	14 yds. [12.8m]
▢ Holly	#31	#27	12 yds. [11m]
▨ Forest	#32	#29	4 yds. [3.7m]
■ Red	#20	#01	1½ yds. [1.4m]
▨ Tangerine	#15	#11	1¼ yds. [1.1m]
▨ Straw	#41	#19	½ yd. [0.5m]
▨ Pumpkin	#50	#12	¼ yd. [0.2m]

STITCH KEY:
- — Backstitch/Straight
- • French Knot

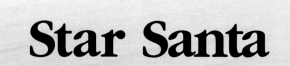

Star Santa

Designed by Michele Wilcox

SIZE
Snugly covers a boutique-style tissue box.

SKILL LEVEL: Easy

MATERIALS
- ❑ Two sheets of 7-count plastic canvas
- ❑ Five gold ⅜" [10mm] jingle bells
- ❑ Sewing needle
- ❑ Craft glue or glue gun
- ❑ #5 pearl cotton or six-strand embroidery floss; for amount see Color Key.
- ❑ Worsted-weight or plastic canvas yarn; for amounts see Color Key.

CUTTING INSTRUCTIONS
A: For top, cut one according to graph.
B: For sides, cut four 30 x 36 holes.
C: For Santa, cut one according to graph.

STITCHING INSTRUCTIONS
1: Using colors and stitches indicated, work pieces according to graphs. With red, Overcast cutout edges of A; with matching colors, Overcast edges of C.
2: Using yarn and pearl cotton or three strands floss in colors and embroidery stitches indicated, embroider facial detail on C as indicated on graph.
3: With red, Whipstitch A and B pieces together, forming Cover; Overcast unfinished bottom edges. With black pearl cotton or floss, sew one jingle bell to each point on C as indicated. Glue C to one Cover side as shown in photo.✿

COLOR KEY: Star Santa

Embroidery floss			AMOUNT
■ Black			¼ yd. [0.2m]

Worsted-weight	Nylon Plus™	Need-loft®	YARN AMOUNT
■ Navy	#45	#31	30 yds. [27.4m]
■ Tangerine	#15	#11	30 yds. [27.4m]
■ Red	#20	#01	15 yds. [13.7m]
■ White	#01	#41	5 yds. [4.6m]
■ Black	#02	#00	2 yds. [1.8m]
■ Coral	#14	#66	1 yd. [0.9m]
■ Xmas Green	#58	#28	1 yd. [0.9m]

STITCH KEY:
- — Backstitch/Straight
- ● French Knot
- ✦ Bell Attachment

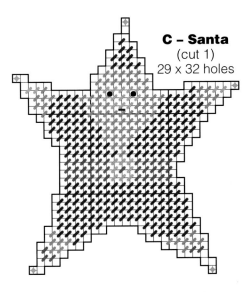

C – Santa
(cut 1)
29 x 32 holes

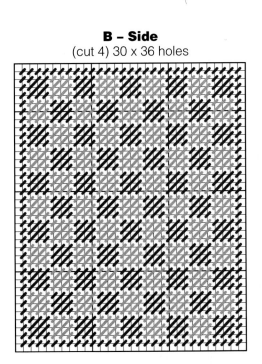

B – Side
(cut 4) 30 x 36 holes

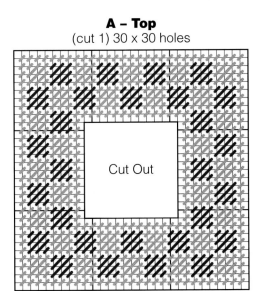

A – Top
(cut 1) 30 x 30 holes

Cut Out

Bell Pull

Designed by Mary T. Cosgrove

SIZE
5" x 13⅝" [12.7cm x 34.6cm].

SKILL LEVEL: Average

MATERIALS
- ❑ One sheet of 7-count plastic canvas
- ❑ Craft glue or glue gun
- ❑ Worsted-weight or plastic canvas yarn; for amounts see Color Key.

CUTTING INSTRUCTIONS
NOTE: Graphs continued on page 14.
A: For base, cut one according to graph.
B: For tops #1-#3, cut one each according to graphs.

STITCHING INSTRUCTIONS
1: Using colors and stitches indicated, work pieces according to graphs. With colors indicated on graphs, Overcast edges of B pieces as indicated.
2: Whipstitch pieces together as indicated and according to Bell Pull Assembly Diagram on page 14.
NOTE: Cut one 9" [22.9cm] length of each yarn color.
3: Tie each cut strand into a bow and trim ends as desired; glue one bow to each bell as shown in photo. Hang as desired.✻

B – Top #1 (cut 1) 30 x 30 holes

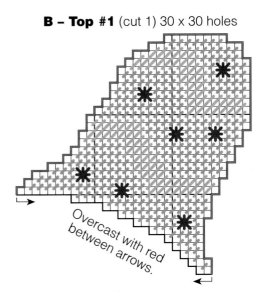

Overcast with red between arrows.

B – Top #2 (cut 1) 30 x 30 holes

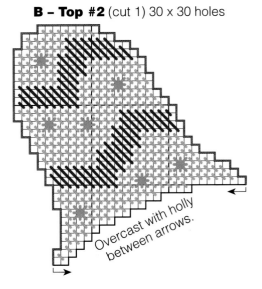

Overcast with holly between arrows.

COLOR KEY: Bell Pull

	Worsted-weight	Nylon Plus™	Need-loft®	YARN AMOUNT
▨	Gold	#27	#17	22 yds. [20.1m]
▨	Holly	#31	#27	22 yds. [20.1m]
■	Red	#20	#01	22 yds. [20.1m]

ATTACHMENT KEY:
- — Top #1
- — Top #2
- — Top #3

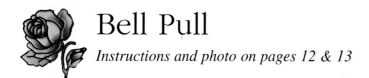

Bell Pull

Instructions and photo on pages 12 & 13

A – Base (cut 1) 34 x 90 holes

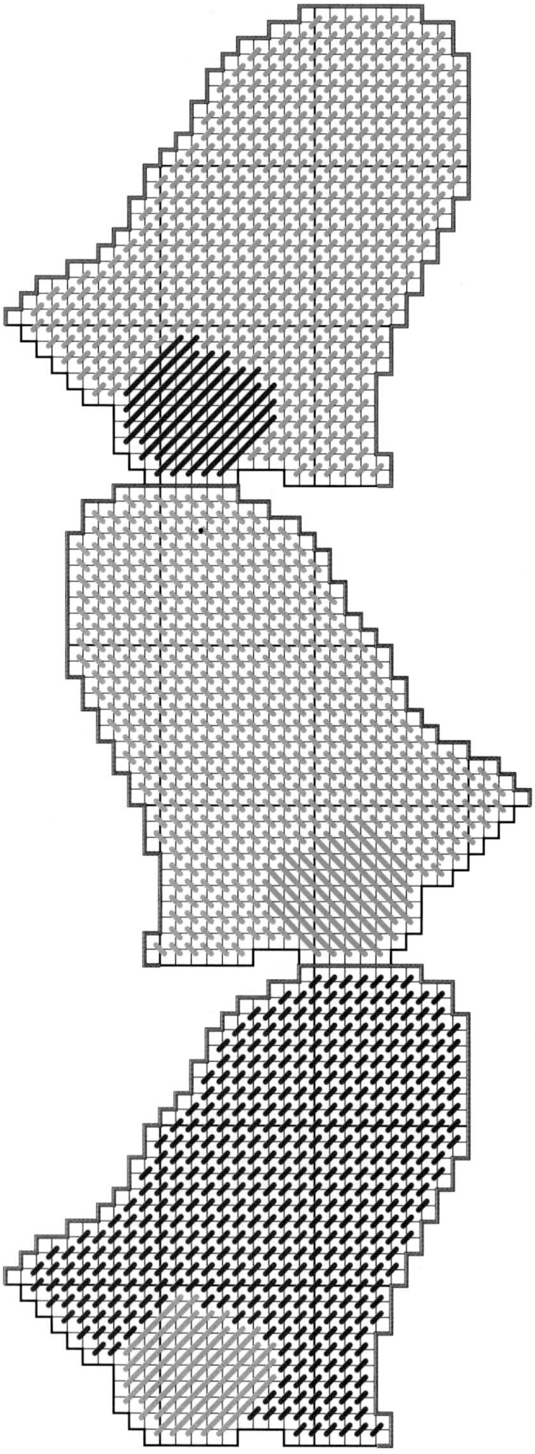

B – Top #3 (cut 1) 30 x 30 holes

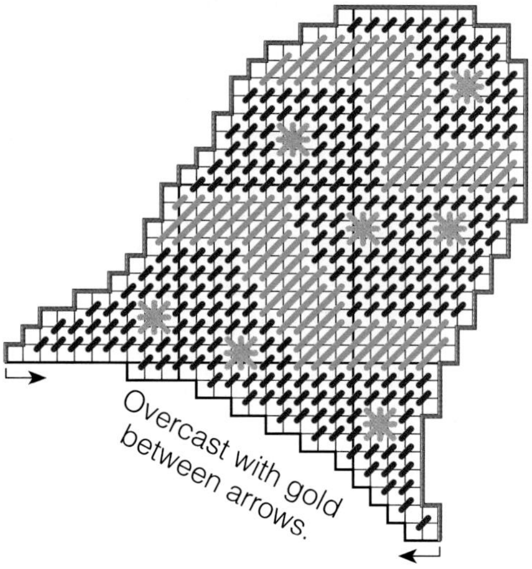
Overcast with gold between arrows.

Bell Pull Assembly Diagram

(Pieces are shown in different colors for contrast.)

Step 1:
For each Bell, holding wrong side of one B to corresponding area on right side of A, with red for #1, holly for #2 and gold for #3, Whipstitch together.

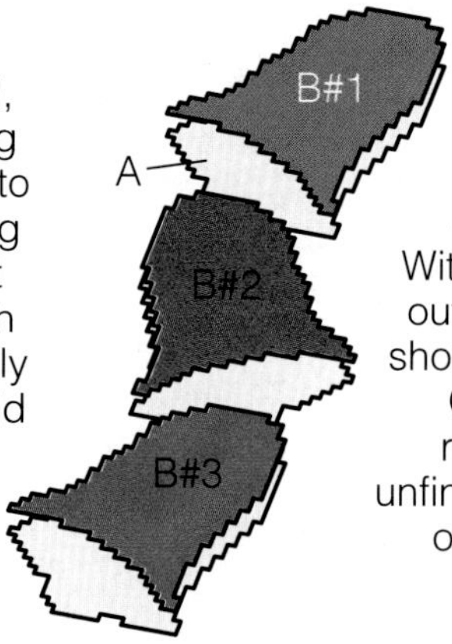
B#1
A
B#2
B#3

Step 2:
With matching outer color as shown in photo, Overcast remaining unfinished edges of A piece.

COLOR KEY: Bell Pull

	Worsted-weight	Nylon Plus™	Need-loft®	YARN AMOUNT
■	Gold	#27	#17	22 yds. [20.1m]
■	Holly	#31	#27	22 yds. [20.1m]
■	Red	#20	#01	22 yds. [20.1m]

ATTACHMENT KEY:

- Top #1
- Top #2
- Top #3

INSTRUCTIONS ON NEXT PAGE

Quilt Classic Trio

Designed by Pam Bull

Quilt Classic Trio

Photo on page 15

SIZES

Heart Box is 6" across x 2½" tall [15.2cm x 6.4cm]; each Coaster is 3½" square [8.9cm]; Coaster Holder is 1¾" x 4⅛" x 2" tall [4.4cm x 10.5cm x 5.1cm].

SKILL LEVEL: Challenging

MATERIALS

❑ Two Uniek® Crafts 6" [15.2cm] plastic canvas heart shapes
❑ One sheet of 7-count plastic canvas
❑ 7" square [17.8cm] piece of ⅛" [3mm] corkboard
❑ Three white 9" x 12" [22.9cm x 30.5cm] sheets of felt
❑ Craft glue or glue gun
❑ Worsted-weight or plastic canvas yarn; for amounts see Color Key.

CUTTING INSTRUCTIONS

A: For Heart Box lid top, use one heart shape.
B: For Heart Box lid side pieces, cut two 5 x 65 holes (no graph).
C: For Heart Box sides, cut two 15 x 62 holes (no graph).
D: For Heart Box bottom, cut one from remaining heart shape according to graph.
E: For Coasters, cut four 23 x 23 holes.
F: For Coaster Holder sides #1 and #2, cut two (one for #1 and one for #2) 13 x 27 holes.
G: For Coaster Holder ends #1 and #2, cut two (one for #1 and one for #2) 10 x 13 holes.
H: For Coaster Holder bottom, cut one 10 x 27 holes (no graph).
I: For Heart Box linings, using A and D pieces as patterns, cut one for lid and two for box bottom from felt ⅛" [3mm] smaller at all edges.
J: For Coaster linings, using E pieces as patterns, cut one each from corkboard ⅛" smaller at all edges.
K: For Coaster Holder linings, using F-H

pieces as patterns, cut one each for sides and ends and two for bottom from felt ⅛" smaller at all edges.

STITCHING INSTRUCTIONS

NOTE: D and H pieces are not worked.
1: Using colors and stitches indicated, work A and E-G pieces according to graphs; work C pieces according to Heart Box Side Stitch Pattern Guide. Using eggshell and Slanted Gobelin Stitch over narrow width, work B pieces. With violet, Overcast edges of E pieces.
2: With eggshell, Whipstitch A-D pieces together according to Heart Box Assembly Diagram. With violet, Whipstitch F-H pieces together as indicated on graphs and according to Coaster Holder Assembly Illustration; Overcast unfinished edges.
3: Glue linings to wrong side of corresponding canvas pieces. (**NOTE:** For Heart Box and Coaster Holder bottoms, glue one lining to each side of corresponding bottom piece.)✳

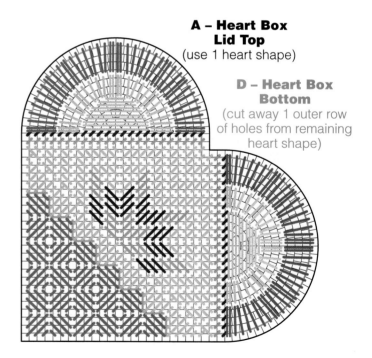

A – Heart Box Lid Top
(use 1 heart shape)

D – Heart Box Bottom
(cut away 1 outer row of holes from remaining heart shape)

E – Coaster
(cut 4) 23 x 23 holes

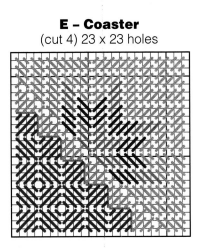

F – Coaster Holder Side #1
(cut 1) 13 x 27 holes

Whipstitch to G#2.

Whipstitch to G#1.

F – Coaster Holder Side #2
(cut 1) 13 x 27 holes

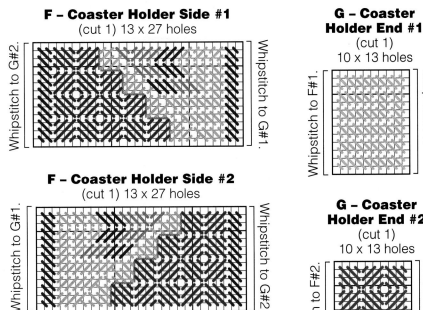

Whipstitch to G#1.

Whipstitch to G#2.

G – Coaster Holder End #1
(cut 1)
10 x 13 holes

Whipstitch to F#1.

Whipstitch to F#2.

G – Coaster Holder End #2
(cut 1)
10 x 13 holes

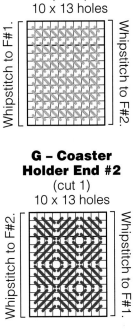

Whipstitch to F#2.

Whipstitch to F#1.

Coaster Holder Assembly Illustration
(Pieces are shown in different colors for contrast; gray denotes wrong side.)

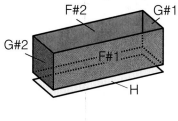

F#2   G#1

G#2

F#1

H

COLOR KEY: Quilt Classic Trio

	Worsted-weight	Nylon Plus™	Need-loft®	YARN AMOUNT
	Eggshell	#24	#39	76 yds. [69.5m]
	Teal Blue	#08	#50	34 yds. [31.1m]
	Violet	#49	#04	27 yds. [24.7m]
	Camel	#34	#43	18 yds. [16.5m]

Heart Box Side Stitch Pattern Guide

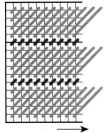

Continue established pattern across each entire piece.

Heart Box Assembly Diagram
(Pieces are shown in different colors for contrast; gray denotes wrong side.)

Step 1: Whipstitch short ends of B pieces together; repeat to join C pieces.

Lid

B

A

Box

C

D

C

Step 3: Overcast unfinished edges of lid and box.

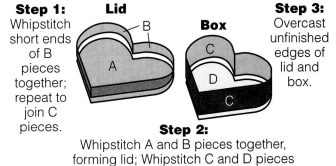

Step 2: Whipstitch A and B pieces together, forming lid; Whipstitch C and D pieces together, forming box.

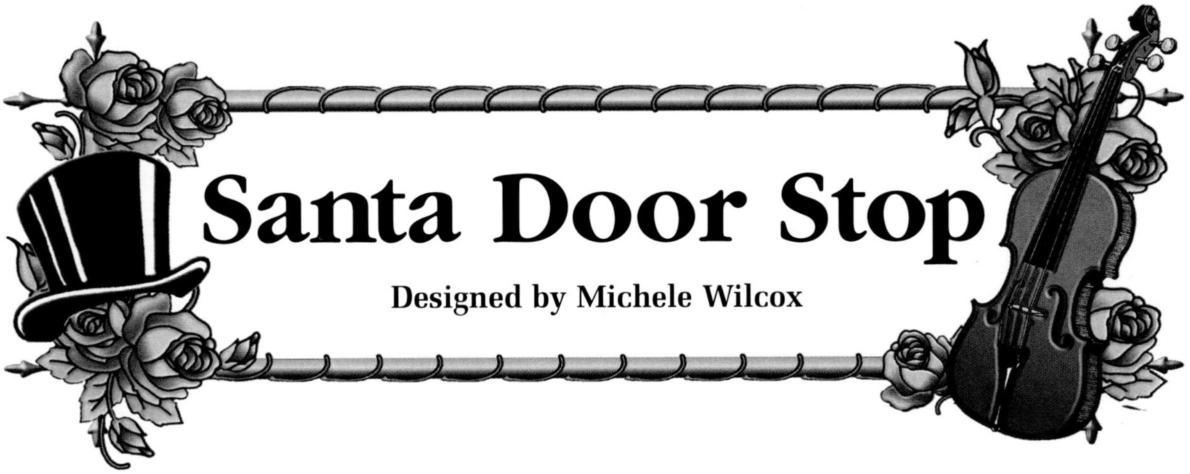

Santa Door Stop

Designed by Michele Wilcox

SIZE

2½" x 7¾" x 4" tall [6.4cm x 19.7cm x 10.2cm], not including embellishments.

SKILL LEVEL: Average

MATERIALS

- ❑ Two sheets of 7-count plastic canvas
- ❑ Five Uniek® plastic canvas star shapes
- ❑ Brick or a zip-close bag filled with gravel or other weighting material
- ❑ 1 yd. [0.9m] of green 22-gauge floral wire
- ❑ Marker
- ❑ Craft glue or glue gun
- ❑ #5 pearl cotton or six-strand embroidery floss; for amount see Color Key.
- ❑ Worsted-weight or plastic canvas yarn; for amounts see Color Key.

CUTTING INSTRUCTIONS

NOTE: Graphs continued on page 20.

A: For motif, cut one according to graph.

B: For large stars, cut two from star shapes according to graph.

C: For medium stars, cut two from star shapes according to graph.

D: For small star, cut one from remaining star shape according to graph.

E: For Cover sides, cut two 26 x 51 holes (no graph).

F: For Cover ends, cut two 16 x 26 holes (no graph).

G: For Cover top and bottom, cut two (one for top and one for bottom) 16 x 51 holes (no graph).

STITCHING INSTRUCTIONS

1: Using colors and stitches indicated, work A-D pieces according to graphs; work E-G pieces according to Cover Stitch Pattern Guide. With matching colors, Overcast edges of A-D pieces.

2: Using pearl cotton or six strands floss and French Knot, embroider eyes on A as indicated on graph.

3: For Cover, with denim, Whipstitch E-G pieces together according to Cover Assembly Illustration, inserting weighting material before closing.

NOTES: Cut four 9" [22.9cm] lengths of floral wire. For each coil, wrap one wire around marker; slide coil off marker.

4: Setting one large star aside, thread one end of each coil through each remaining star as indicated; twist ends around wire to secure (see photo).

5: Glue coils to back of motif; glue motif and remaining large star to one side of Cover as shown or as desired.❇

A – Motif (cut 1) 29 x 49 holes

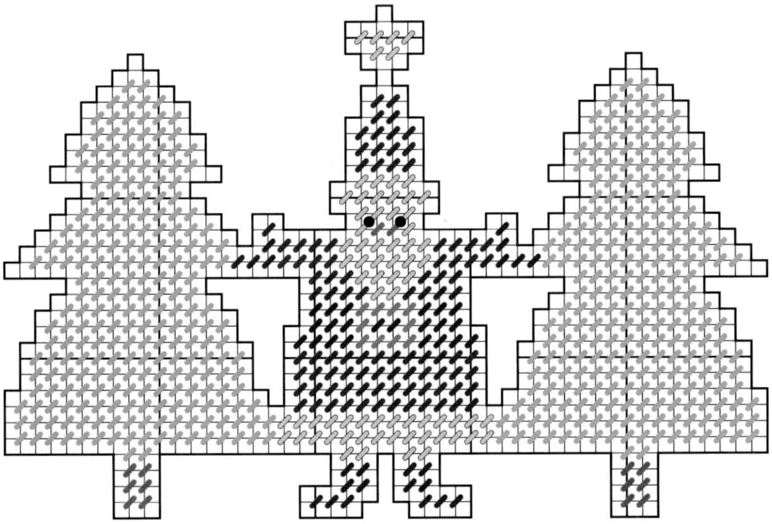

COLOR KEY: Christmas Door Stop

#5 pearl cotton or floss			AMOUNT
Black			1/4 yd. [0.2m]
Worsted-weight	**Nylon Plus™**	**Need-loft®**	**YARN AMOUNT**
Denim	#06	#33	75 yds. [68.6m]
Mint	#30	#24	13 yds. [11.9m]
Tangerine	#15	#11	8 yds. [7.3m]
Black	#02	#00	4 yds. [3.7m]
Xmas Red	#19	#02	4 yds. [3.7m]
White	#01	#41	3 yds. [2.7m]
Camel	#34	#43	1 yd. [0.9m]
Coral	#14	#66	1/2 yd. [0.5m]

STITCH KEY:

- ● French Knot
- ✦ Wire Attachment

Santa Door Stop
Photo and instructions on pages 18 & 19

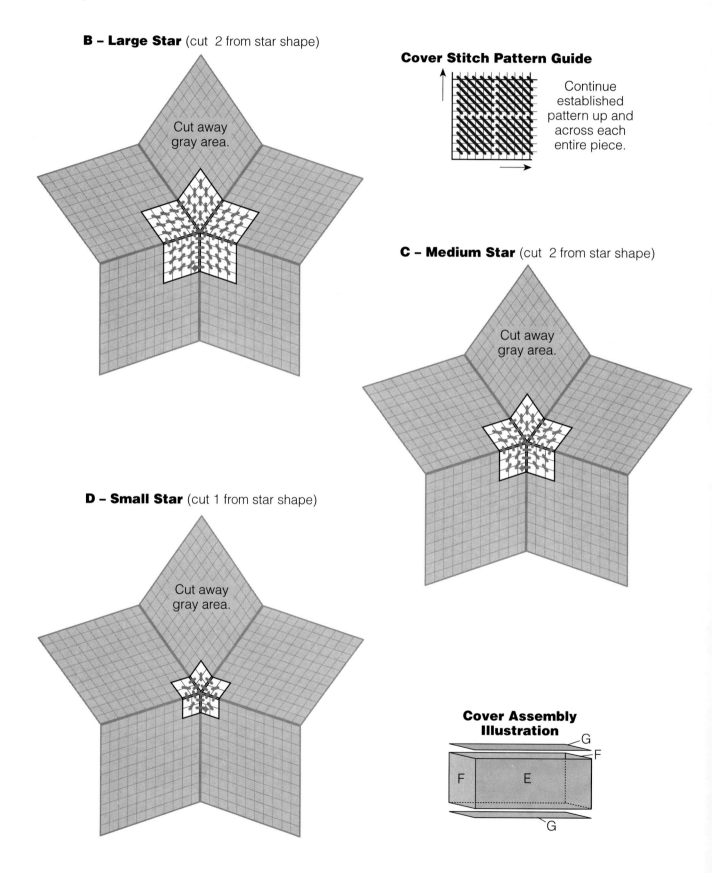

B – Large Star (cut 2 from star shape)

Cut away
gray area.

Cover Stitch Pattern Guide

Continue
established
pattern up and
across each
entire piece.

C – Medium Star (cut 2 from star shape)

Cut away
gray area.

D – Small Star (cut 1 from star shape)

Cut away
gray area.

**Cover Assembly
Illustration**

G
F
F
E
G

INSTRUCTIONS ON NEXT PAGE

Patchwork Desk Trio

Designed by Nancy Marshall

Patchwork Desk Trio

Photo on page 21

SIZES

Letter Box is 4" x $9\frac{7}{8}$" x $3\frac{7}{8}$" tall [10.2cm x 25.1cm x 9.8cm]; Note Holder is 4" square x $2\frac{3}{8}$" tall [10.2cm x 6cm]; Pencil Box is $2\frac{3}{8}$" square x $3\frac{7}{8}$" tall [6cm x 9.8cm].

SKILL LEVEL: Average

MATERIALS

- ❑ Three sheets of 7-count plastic canvas
- ❑ Seven $\frac{1}{2}$" [13mm] and eight $\frac{3}{4}$" [19mm] assorted-color decorative buttons
- ❑ 18" x 22" [45.7cm x 55.9cm] piece of $\frac{1}{8}$" [3mm] poster board
- ❑ 20" x 24" [50.8cm x 61cm] piece of dk. blue cotton fabric
- ❑ Quilting needle (optional)
- ❑ Craft glue or glue gun
- ❑ Worsted-weight or plastic canvas yarn; for amounts see Color Key.

CUTTING INSTRUCTIONS

A: For Letter Holder sides, cut two 25 x 65 holes.
B: For Letter Holder ends, cut two 25 x 25 holes.
C: For Letter Holder bottom, cut one 25 x 65 holes (no graph).
D: For Note Holder cutout side, cut one according to graph.
E: For Note Holder solid sides, cut three 15 x 25 holes.
F: For Note Holder bottom, cut one 25 x 25 holes (no graph).
G: For Pencil Box sides, cut four 15 x 25 holes.
H: For Pencil Box bottom, cut one 15 x 15 holes (no graph).
I: For linings, using A-H pieces as patterns, cut one each from poster board $\frac{1}{4}$" [6mm] smaller at all edges.
J: For lining covers, using I pieces as patterns, cut one each from fabric $\frac{1}{2}$" [13mm] larger at all edges.

STITCHING INSTRUCTIONS

NOTE: C, F and H pieces are not worked.

1: Using colors and stitches indicated, work A, B, D, E and G pieces according to graphs. Using cinnamon and Backstitch, embroider detail on worked pieces as indicated on graphs.
2: Glue, or with quilting needle and yellow yarn, sew one $\frac{3}{4}$" button to each ◆ hole on A and B pieces as indicated; repeat to attach $\frac{1}{2}$" buttons on E and G pieces as indicated.
3: With cinnamon, Whipstitch pieces together according to corresponding assembly illustrations; Overcast unfinished edges of Letter Holder and Pencil Box. With cinnamon for top edges and with matching colors as shown in photo for notched edges, Overcast unfinished edges of Note Holder.
4: For each lining, cover one I piece with matching J piece; glue ends of fabric to poster board to secure. Glue linings inside holders and box at corresponding sides, ends and bottoms.❋

A – Letter Holder Side (cut 2) 25 x 65 holes

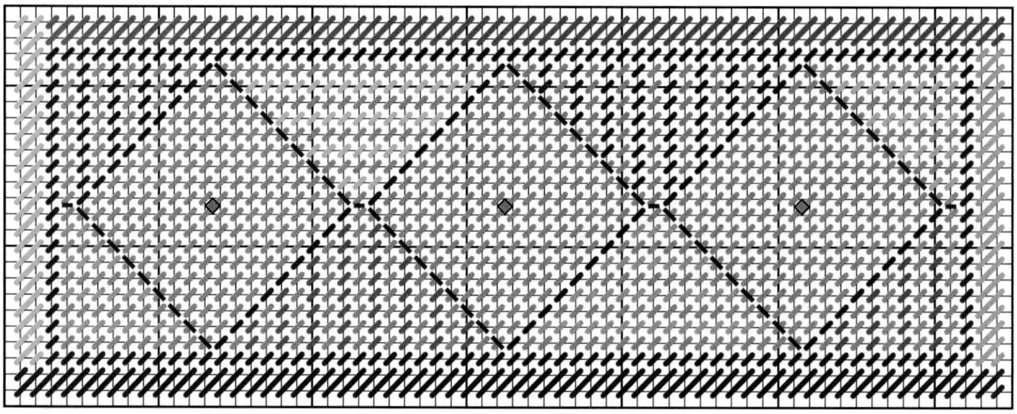

B – Letter Holder End
(cut 2) 25 x 25 holes

D – Note Holder Cutout Side
(cut 1) 15 x 25 holes

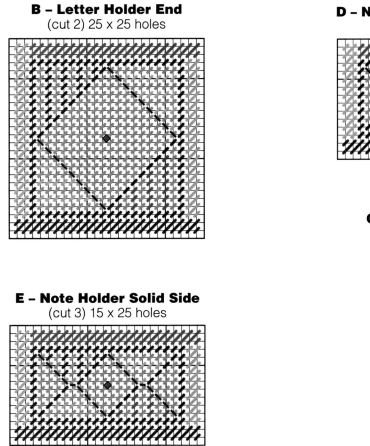

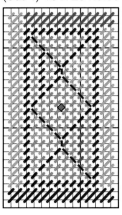

E – Note Holder Solid Side
(cut 3) 15 x 25 holes

G – Pencil Box Side
(cut 4) 15 x 25 holes

COLOR KEY: Patchwork Desk Trio

	Worsted-weight	Nylon Plus™	Need-loft®	YARN AMOUNT
	Sandstone	#47	#16	42 yds. [38.4m]
	Cinnamon	#44	#14	40 yds. [36.6m]
	Navy	#45	#31	14 yds. [12.8m]
	Red	#20	#01	14 yds. [12.8m]
	Yellow	#26	#57	13 yds. [11.9m]
	Mint	#30	#24	12 yds. [11m]

ATTACHMENT/PLACEMENT KEY:
◆ Button

Assembly Illustrations
(Pieces are shown in different colors for contrast; gray denotes wrong side.)

Letter Holder

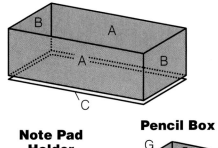

Note Pad Holder

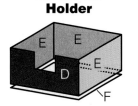

Pencil Box

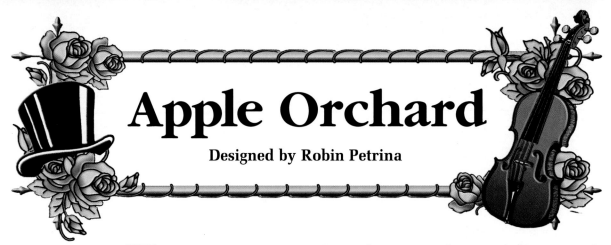

Apple Orchard

Designed by Robin Petrina

SIZE

Each apple is 4" x 4¼" [10.2cm x 10.8cm], with a 2¼" x 2½" [5.7cm x 6.4cm] photo window.

SKILL LEVEL: Easy

MATERIALS

- ❑ One sheet of 7-count plastic canvas
- ❑ Craft glue or glue gun
- ❑ Worsted-weight or plastic canvas yarn; for amounts see Color Key.

CUTTING INSTRUCTIONS

A: For fronts, cut three according to graph.
B: For backs, cut three according to graph.
C: For leaves, cut three according to graph.

STITCHING INSTRUCTIONS

NOTE: B pieces are not worked.

1: Using colors and stitches indicated, work A (one on opposite side of canvas) and C pieces according to graphs; with crimson, Overcast cutout edges of A pieces; with Xmas green, Overcast edges of C pieces.

2: For each apple, holding one B to wrong side of one A, with crimson, Whipstitch together as indicated on graphs; with matching colors, Overcast unfinished edges of front.

3: Glue one leaf to each apple, and glue apples together as shown in photo or as desired. Hang or display as desired.❋

COLOR KEY: Apple Orchard

Worsted-weight	Nylon Plus™	Need-loft®	YARN AMOUNT
Crimson	#53	#42	21 yds. [19.2m]
Xmas Green	#58	#28	6 yds. [5.5m]
Brown	#36	#15	4 yds. [3.7m]

C – Leaf
(cut 3)
5 x 10 holes

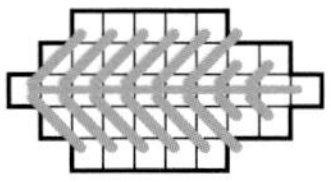

A – Front
(cut 3) 26 x 27 holes

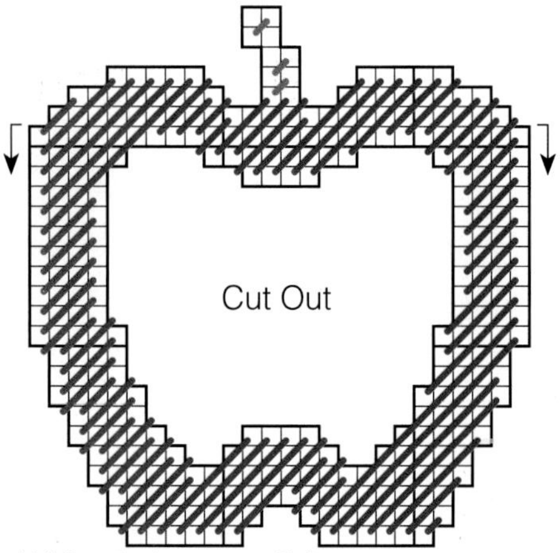

Whipstitch to one B between arrows.

B – Back
(cut 3) 24 x 26 holes

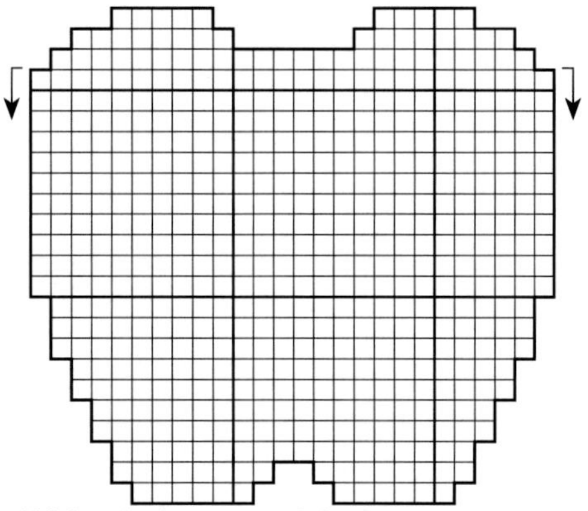

Whipstitch to one A between arrows.

INSTRUCTIONS ON
NEXT PAGE

Yuletide
Decor

Designed by Mike Vickery

Yuletide Decor

Photo on pages 26 & 27

SIZES

Stocking is 11⅛" x 15" [28.3cm x 38.1cm], not including hanger; stitched area of Cardinal is 11½" x 11½" [29.2cm x 29.2cm]; stitched area of Violin is 10" x 10" [25.4cm x 25.4cm]; stitched area of Cherubs is 12" x 12" [30.5cm x 30.5cm]; stitched area of Angel is 12" x 12" [30.5cm x 30.5cm].

SKILL LEVEL: Average

MATERIALS FOR ALL

❑ Six 13½" x 21½" [34.3cm x 54.6cm] sheets of 7-count plastic canvas
❑ 33 red and six green 6mm round faceted beads
❑ 27 red 4mm round faceted beads
❑ Sewing needle and monofilament fishing line
❑ Frame, or mat and frame of choice
❑ Fine (#8) metallic braid or metallic thread; for amount see Violin Color Key on page 32.
❑ Medium (#16) metallic braid or metallic cord; for amount see Stocking Color Key.
❑ Six-strand embroidery floss; for amount see individual Color Keys on pages 29-33.
❑ Worsted-weight or plastic canvas yarn; for amounts see individual Color Keys.

CUTTING INSTRUCTIONS

A: For Stocking front and back, cut two (one for front and one for back) according to graph.
B: For Cardinal, Violin, Cherubs and Angel Portraits, use one sheet of canvas per portrait.

STITCHING INSTRUCTIONS

1: For Stocking, using colors indicated and Continental Stitch, work one A for front (work letters of choice to spell name according to Alphabet Graph) according to graph; fill in uncoded areas of front A and work back A on opposite side of canvas using baby blue and Continental Stitch.

2: Using yarn (Separate into individual plies, if desired.) and six strands floss in colors and embroidery stitches indicated, embroider detail on front A as indicated on graph. With fishing line, sew 6mm beads to front A as indicated.

3: Holding A pieces wrong sides together, with white for cuff edges and with baby blue (see photo), Whipstitch together as indicated; with white, Overcast unfinished top edges. Hang as desired.

4: For Portraits, using colors indicated and Continental Stitch, work B (center design on canvas) pieces according to graphs; do not Overcast edges. Using yarn (Separate into individual plies, if desired.), fine metallic braid and six strands floss in colors and embroidery stitches indicated, embroider detail on B pieces as indicated, securing couching stitches on Violin with fishing line as you work.

5: With fishing line, sew 4mm beads to Cardinal B as indicated and remaining 6mm beads to Violin, Cherubs and Angel B pieces as indicated. Frame each Portrait as desired.✣

Alphabet Graph

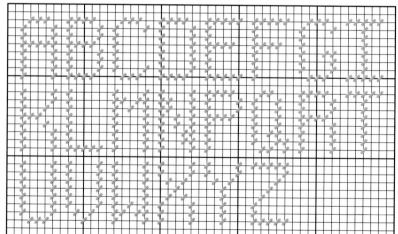

COLOR KEY: Stocking

Embroidery floss			AMOUNT
■ Dk. Gray			12 yds. [11m]

Med. metallic braid or cord		Kreinik	AMOUNT
▨ Star Yellow		#091	¹/₄ yd. [0.2m]

Worsted-weight	Nylon Plus™	Need-loft®	YARN AMOUNT
□ Baby Blue	#05	#36	4 oz. [113.4g]
▨ White	#01	#41	25 yds. [22.9m]
■ Camel	#34	#43	15 yds. [13.7m]
▨ Yellow	#26	#57	15 yds. [13.7m]
▨ Holly	#31	#27	10 yds. [9.1m]
▨ Gold	#27	#17	8 yds. [7.3m]
▨ Sandstone	#47	#16	8 yds. [7.3m]
▨ Forest	#32	#29	6 yds. [5.5m]
■ Crimson	#53	#42	4 yds. [3.7m]
▨ Red	#20	#01	4 yds. [3.7m]
▨ Xmas Red	#19	#02	4 yds. [3.7m]
▨ Black	#02	#00	3 yds. [2.7m]
■ Brown	#36	#15	3 yds. [2.7m]
▨ Fern	#57	#23	3 yds. [2.7m]
▨ Silver	–	#37	2 yds. [1.8m]
▨ Turquoise	#03	#54	2 yds. [1.8m]
▨ Beige	#43	#40	1 yd. [0.9m]
▨ Flesh Tone	–	#56	1 yd. [0.9m]
■ Gray	#23	#38	1 yd. [0.9m]

STITCH KEY:
- — Backstitch/Straight
- ● French Knot
- ✦ 6mm Red Bead Attachment

Whipstitch between arrows.

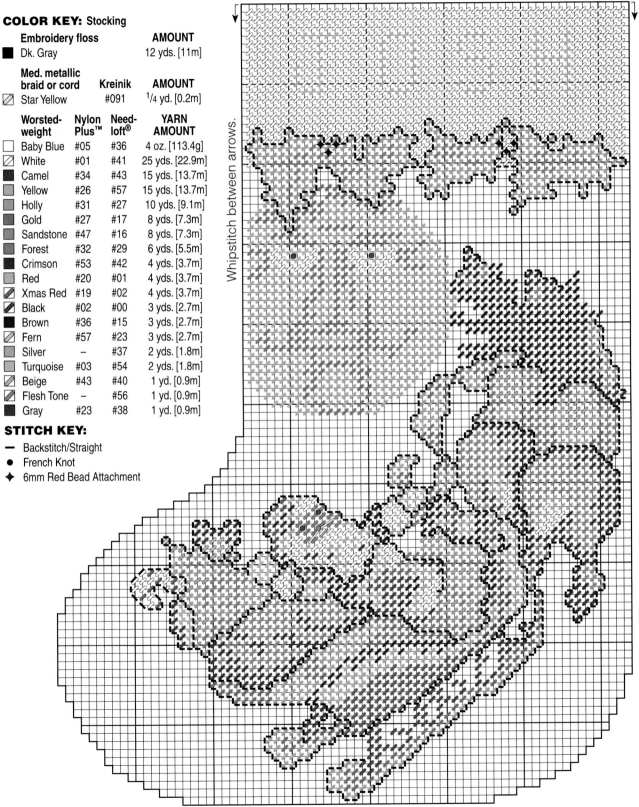

Yuletide Decor

Instructions on page 28

COLOR KEY: Cardinal

Embroidery floss			AMOUNT
■ Dk. Gray			8 yds. [7.3m]

Worsted-weight	Nylon Plus™	Need-loft®	YARN AMOUNT
Baby Blue	#05	#36	56 yds. [51.2m]
⊘ White	#01	#41	15 yds. [13.7m]
Cerulean	#38	#34	13 yds. [11.9m]

Worsted-weight	Nylon Plus™	Need-loft®	YARN AMOUNT
Holly	#31	#27	8 yds. [7.3m]
Gray	#23	#38	7 yds. [6.4m]
Forest	#32	#29	6 yds. [5.5m]
Camel	#34	#43	3 yds. [2.7m]
Fern	#57	#23	3 yds. [2.7m]
Silver	–	#37	3 yds. [2.7m]
■ Crimson	#53	#42	2 yds. [1.8m]

Worsted-weight	Nylon Plus™	Need-loft®	YARN AMOUNT
◪ Pumpkin	#50	#12	2 yds. [1.8m]
Red	#20	#01	2 yds. [1.8m]
Tangerine	#15	#11	2 yds. [1.8m]
Beige	#43	#40	1 yd. [0.9m]
Black	#02	#00	1 yd. [0.9m]
◪ Xmas Red	#19	#02	1 yd. [0.9m]
⊘ Yellow	#26	#57	1 yd. [0.9m]

STITCH KEY:

— Backstitch/Straight

✦ 4mm Bead Attachment

B – Cardinal (cut 1)

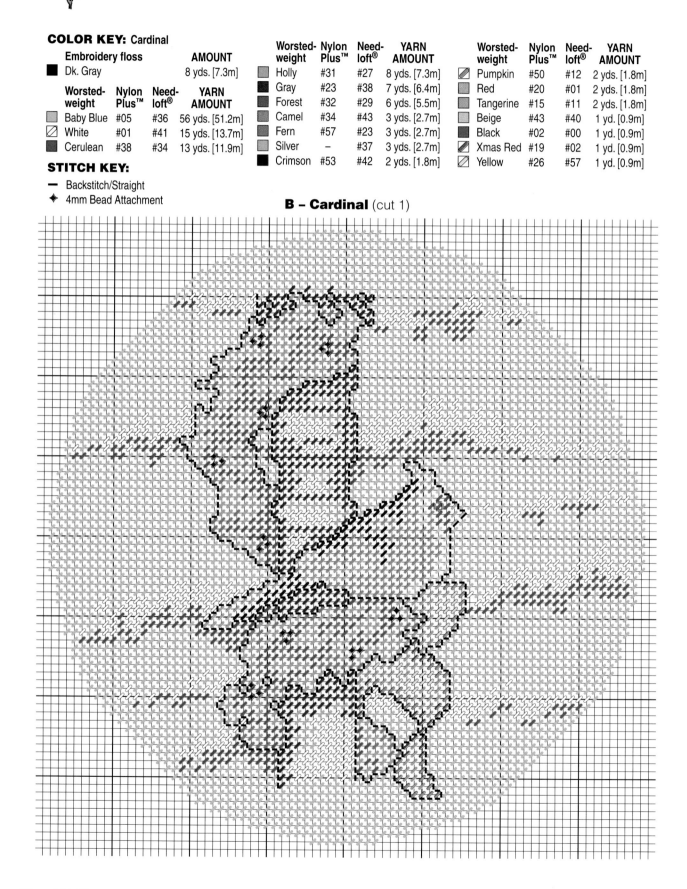

COLOR KEY: Cherubs

Embroidery floss			AMOUNT
■ Dk. Gray			10 yds. [9.1m]

Worsted-weight	Nylon Plus™	Need-loft®	YARN AMOUNT
▨ Baby Blue	#05	#36	83 yds. [75.9m]
▨ Flesh Tone	–	#56	12 yds. [11m]

Worsted-weight	Nylon Plus™	Need-loft®	YARN AMOUNT
▨ Baby Pink	#10	#08	8 yds. [7.3m]
▨ Holly	#31	#27	7 yds. [6.4m]
▨ Forest	#32	#29	6 yds. [5.5m]
▨ Xmas Red	#19	#02	5 yds. [4.6m]
■ Crimson	#53	#42	4 yds. [3.7m]
■ Gray	#23	#38	4 yds. [3.7m]

Worsted-weight	Nylon Plus™	Need-loft®	YARN AMOUNT
■ Fern	#57	#23	3 yds. [2.7m]
■ Silver	–	#37	3 yds. [2.7m]
▨ White	#01	#41	3 yds. [2.7m]
▨ Gold	#27	#17	2 yds. [1.8m]
▨ Red	#20	#01	2 yds. [1.8m]
▨ Yellow	#26	#57	2 yds. [1.8m]

STITCH KEY:

- — Backstitch/Straight
- ● French Knot
- ◇ 6mm Green Bead Attachment
- ✦ 6mm Red Bead Attachment

B – Cherubs (cut 1)

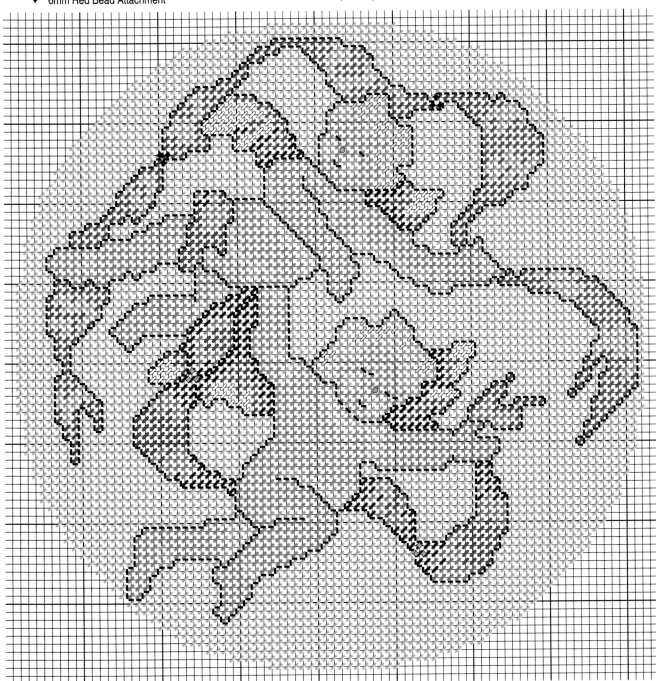

Yuletide Decor
Instructions on page 28

COLOR KEY: Violin

Embroidery floss **AMOUNT**
■ Dk. Gray 10 yds. [9.1m]

Fine metallic braid or thread Kreinik **AMOUNT**
■ Silver #001 6 yds. [5.5m]

Worsted-weight	Nylon Plus™	Need-loft®	YARN AMOUNT
Baby Blue #05	#36		48 yds. [43.9m]

	Worsted-weight	Nylon Plus™	Need-loft®	YARN AMOUNT
	Sandstone	#47	#16	10 yds. [9.1m]
	Yellow	#26	#57	8 yds. [7.3m]
	Beige	#43	#40	6 yds. [5.5m]
	Black	#02	#00	6 yds. [5.5m]
	Camel	#34	#43	6 yds. [5.5m]
	Fern	#57	#23	6 yds. [5.5m]

	Worsted-weight	Nylon Plus™	Need-loft®	YARN AMOUNT
	Forest	#32	#29	6 yds. [5.5m]
	Holly	#31	#27	5 yds. [4.6m]
	Gray	#23	#38	3 yds. [2.7m]
	Pumpkin	#50	#12	3 yds. [2.7m]
	Tangerine	#15	#11	3 yds. [2.7m]
	Gold	#27	#17	2 yds. [1.8m]

STITCH KEY:
— Backstitch/Straight
— Couching
✦ 6mm Red Bead Attachment

B – Violin (cut 1)

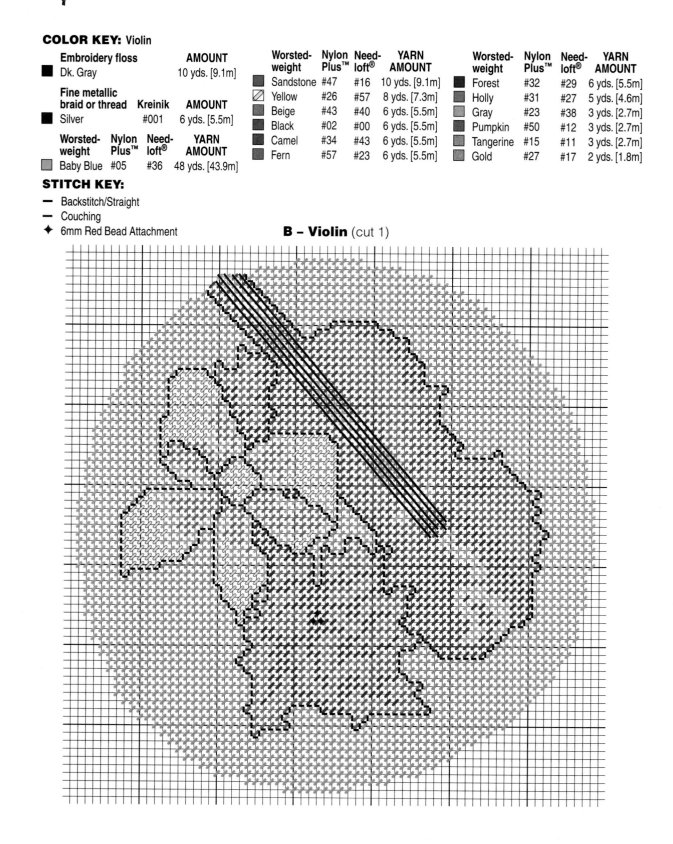

COLOR KEY: Angel

Embroidery floss   **AMOUNT**

■ Dk. Gray   14 yds. [12.8m]

	Worsted-weight	Nylon Plus™	Need-loft®	YARN AMOUNT
■	Baby Blue	#05	#36	80 yds. [73.2m]
■	Fern	#57	#23	15 yds. [13.7m]
■	Holly	#31	#27	14 yds. [12.8m]
■	Forest	#32	#29	8 yds. [7.3m]

	Worsted-weight	Nylon Plus™	Need-loft®	YARN AMOUNT
⊘	Sail Blue	#04	#35	5 yds. [4.6m]
▨	Silver	–	#37	5 yds. [4.6m]
⊘	White	#01	#41	5 yds. [4.6m]
⊘	Xmas Red	#19	#02	4 yds. [3.7m]
■	Crimson	#53	#42	3 yds. [2.7m]
▨	Flesh Tone	–	#56	3 yds. [2.7m]

	Worsted-weight	Nylon Plus™	Need-loft®	YARN AMOUNT
■	Gray	#23	#38	3 yds. [2.7m]
■	Turquoise	#03	#54	3 yds. [2.7m]
■	Red	#20	#01	2 yds. [1.8m]
■	Gold	#27	#17	1 yd. [0.9m]
⊘	Yellow	#26	#57	1 yd. [0.9m]
■	Cinnamon	#44	#14	1/4 yd. [0.2m]

STITCH KEY:

— Backstitch/Straight

✦ 6mm Red Bead Attachment

B – Angel (cut 1)

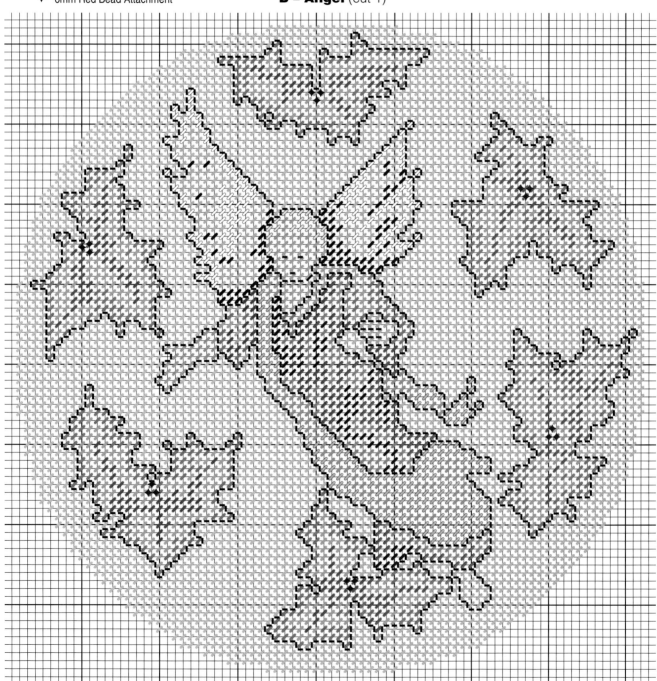

Farm Friends

Cultivate a festival of fun with the adorable critters and smiling faces you'll find in this happy harvest of designs. City dwellers and country cousins alike will flock to your door with bushels of praise for these handpicked selections. Never be fenced in by ordinary projects again when you hatch this batch of frolicking friends to share your home. Your creativity will rise and shine to new heights with ideas for tissue covers, centerpieces, coasters, and more -- all guaranteed to produce loads of laughs. Whether you prefer feathers or fur, you'll enjoy this passel of pasteurized playmates so much, wild horses couldn't drag you away!

Harvest Scarecrow

Designed by Celia Lange Designs

SIZE
7" x 11¼" x about 11" tall [17.8cm x 28.6cm x 27.9cm].

SKILL LEVEL: Challenging

MATERIALS
- ❏ Three sheets of 7-count plastic canvas
- ❏ 2½" x 2½" x 5½" [6.4cm x 6.4cm x 14cm] hay bale
- ❏ 9" [22.9cm] of ⅛" [3mm] twine
- ❏ Two 12mm round wiggle eyes
- ❏ One 4" [10.2cm] blue oval tin tub
- ❏ One 1" [2.5cm] artificial crow
- ❏ Assorted miniature pumpkins, squash, fruit, nuts and berries
- ❏ Six or more 1" [2.5cm] silk flower blossoms
- ❏ Two large autumn-color silk leaves
- ❏ 12" [30.5cm] of coat hanger wire
- ❏ Two white ⅜" [10mm] 4-hole buttons
- ❏ 4 yds. [3.7m] natural raffia straw
- ❏ Craft glue or glue gun
- ❏ #3 pearl cotton or six-strand embroidery floss; for amount see Color Key on page 38.
- ❏ Worsted-weight or plastic canvas yarn; for amounts see Color Key.

CUTTING INSTRUCTIONS
NOTE: Graphs on pages 38 and 39.

A: For base, cut one according to graph.

B: For sign front and back, cut two (one for front and one for back) 19 x 27 holes.

C: For post side pieces, cut eight 3 x 41 holes.

D: For post end pieces, cut four 3 x 3 holes.

E: For body front and back, cut two (one for front and one for back) according to graph.

F: For upper legs #1 and #2, cut one each according to graphs.

G: For lower legs #1 and #2, cut one each according to graphs.

H: For shoes #1 and #2, cut one each according to graphs.

I: For hands, cut two according to graph.

J: For sleeve fronts and backs, cut two each according to graphs.

K: For head front and back, cut two (one for front and one for back) according to graph.

L: For hat pieces, cut two according to graph.

STITCHING INSTRUCTIONS

1: Using colors and stitches indicated, work A and C-L (one L on opposite side of canvas) pieces according to graphs; using eggshell and Continental Stitch, work B pieces. With forest for base and sandstone for hands, Overcast edges of A and I pieces; with indicated colors, Overcast indicated edges of E and J-L pieces.

2: Using pearl cotton or six strands floss and yarn (Separate into individual plies, if desired.) in colors and embroidery stitches indicated, embroider detail on one B, one E and one K piece as indicated on graphs for fronts.

3: For sign, with tan, Whipstitch B pieces wrong sides together; for each post, Whipstitch four C and two D pieces together; glue sign between posts (see Sign Assembly Illustration).

4: With pearl cotton or six strands floss, sew buttons to front E as indicated.

5: For body, omitting upper leg attachment edges, with navy for shirt and maple for trousers, Whipstitch unfinished edges of E pieces wrong sides together; Overcast leg attachment edges on back only.

6: With brown for shoe edges and with maple, Whipstitch front E and F-H pieces together as indicated; with matching colors, Overcast edges of legs and shoes.

7: For each sleeve, with navy, Whipstitch unfinished edges of one of each J wrong sides together. For head, with sandstone, Whipstitch unfinished edges of K pieces wrong sides together. For hat, with sundown, Whipstitch unfinished edges of L pieces wrong sides together.

NOTE: Cut raffia into 1"-3" [2.5-7.6cm] pieces.

8: Glue one hand and several short raffia pieces inside cuff of each sleeve; glue one sleeve inside opening on each side of body (see photo). Glue medium raffia pieces inside neck opening on head; glue head over neck area of body. Glue long raffia pieces inside back of hat and remaining pieces to inside of hat front; glue hat

Harvest Scarecrow

Continued from page 37

over head as shown. Trim raffia as desired.

9: Tie twine into a knot around waist for belt; glue eyes to head as shown. Assemble hay bale, wire and scarecrow according to Scarecrow Assembly Diagram. Glue hay bale and sign to base as indicated; glue tub to base near sign and miniatures and florals to assembly as desired or as shown.✳

COLOR KEY: Harvest Scarecrow

	Pearl cotton or floss			AMOUNT
■	Black			2 yds. [1.8m]

	Worsted-weight	Nylon Plus™	Need-loft®	YARN AMOUNT
■	Forest	#32	#29	34 yds. [31.1m]
■	Aqua	#60	#51	22 yds. [20.1m]
□	Eggshell	#24	#39	19 yds. [17.4m]
■	Maple	#35	#13	19 yds. [17.4m]
■	Navy	#45	#31	18 yds. [16.4m]
■	Red	#20	#01	16 yds. [14.6m]
■	Sundown	#16	#10	14 yds. [12.8m]
■	Tan	#33	#18	12 yds. [11m]
■	Sandstone	#47	#16	8 yds. [7.3m]
■	Brown	#36	#15	4 yds. [3.7m]

STITCH KEY:

— Backstitch/Straight
● French Knot
✕ Cross Stitch
○ Button Attachment

PLACEMENT KEY:

□ Hay Bale
□ Post

C – Post Side Piece
(cut 8)
3 x 41 holes

D – Post End Piece
(cut 4)
3 x 3 holes

B – Sign Front & Back
(cut 1 each) 19 x 27 holes

HAPPY HARVEST

Sign Assembly Illustration

D
³⁄₈" [10mm]
Sign
C
C
Post
D

A – Base
(cut 1) 44 x 73 holes

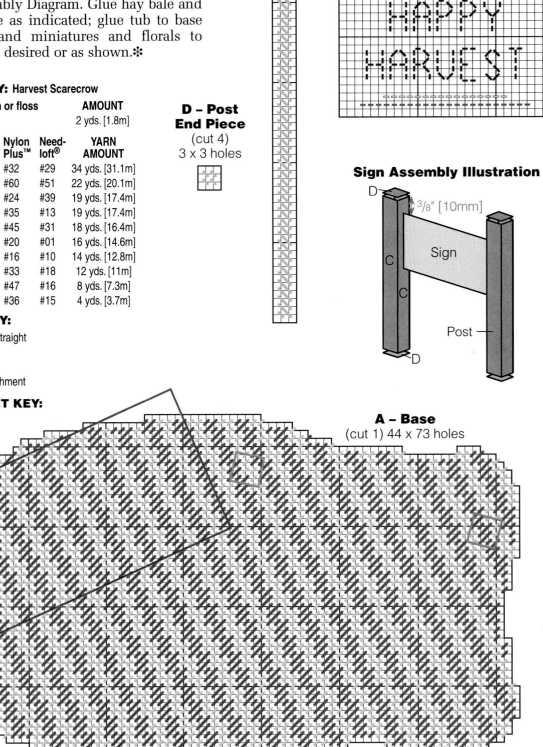

E – Body Front & Back
(cut 1 each) 21 x 29 holes

Overcast with navy.

Overcast with navy.

Whipstitch front to F#1.

Overcast with maple.

Whipstitch front to F#2.

F – Upper Leg #1
(cut 1)
12 x 13 holes

Whipstitch to front E.

Whipstitch to G#1.

F – Upper Leg #2
(cut 1)
12 x 13 holes

Whipstitch to front E.

Whipstitch to G#2.

G – Lower Leg #1
(cut 1)
10 x 18 holes

Whipstitch to F#1.

Whipstitch to H#1.

G – Lower Leg #2
(cut 1)
10 x 18 holes

Whipstitch to F#2.

Whipstitch to H#2.

H – Shoe #1
(cut 1)
7 x 9 holes

Whipstitch to G#1.

H – Shoe #2
(cut 1)
7 x 9 holes

Whipstitch to G#2.

I – Hand
(cut 2)
6 x 10 holes

J – Sleeve Front
(cut 2)
12 x 22 holes

Overcast with red.

J – Sleeve Back
(cut 2)
12 x 22 holes

Overcast with red.

K – Head Front & Back
(cut 1 each) 17 x 18 holes

Overcast with sandstone between arrows.

L – Hat Piece
(cut 2) 13 x 30 holes

Overcast with sundown between arrows.

Scarecrow Assembly Diagram
(Pieces are shown in different colors for contrast; raffia not shown.)

Step 1:
Bend wire in half; push ends up through bottom of bale at center.

1"
[2.5cm]

1 1/2"
[3.8cm]

Wire

Hay Bale

Body Front

Wire

Body Back

Step 2:
Slip one wire between body front and back at each upper leg attachment; sit scarecrow on bale.

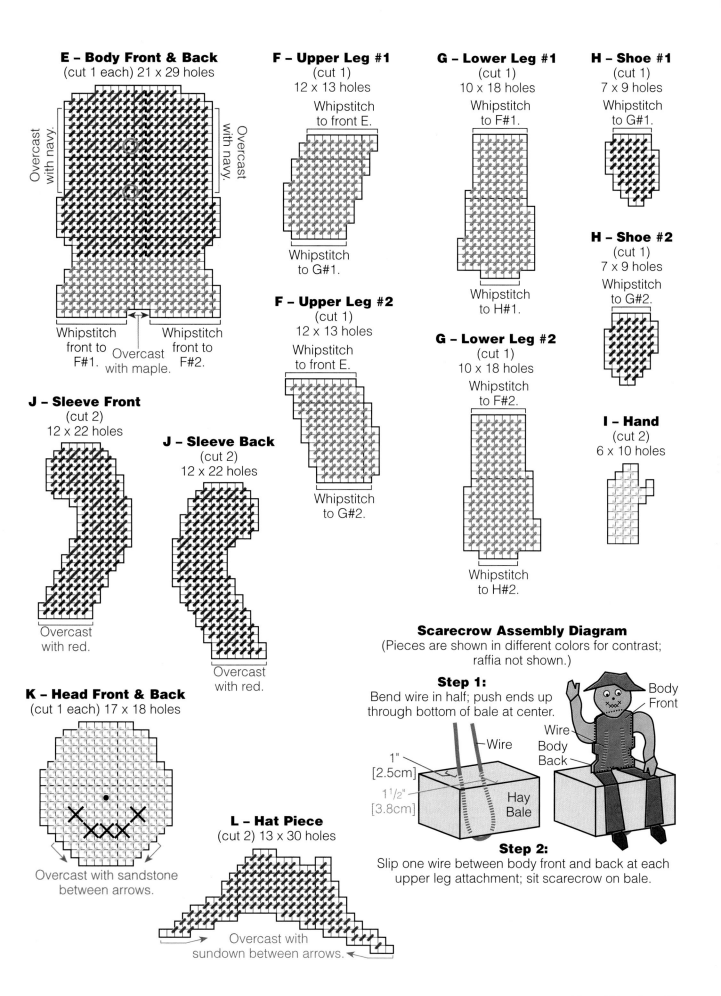

Dog-Gone Treats

Designed by Sandra Miller Maxfield

SIZE
5" square x 5⅞" tall [12.7cm x 15cm], not including handle.

SKILL LEVEL: Average

MATERIALS
- ❏ Two sheets of 7-count plastic canvas
- ❏ Craft glue or glue gun
- ❏ Worsted-weight or plastic canvas yarn; for amounts see Color Key.

CUTTING INSTRUCTIONS
NOTE: Graphs continued on page 42.
A: For box sides, cut four 32 x 37 holes.
B: For box bottom, cut one 32 x 32 holes (no graph).
C: For box lip, cut one according to graph.
D: For lid top, cut one 33 x 33 holes.
E: For lid lip pieces, cut four 2 x 26 holes.
F: For body, cut one according to graph.
G: For arms #1 and #2, cut one each according to graphs.
H: For feet, cut two according to graph.
I: For tail, cut one according to graph.
J: For bones, cut three according to graph.

STITCHING INSTRUCTIONS
NOTE: B and C are not worked.
1: Using colors and stitches indicated, work A and D-J pieces according to graphs; with camel, Overcast edges of F-I pieces.
2: Using colors (Separate into individual plies, if desired.) indicated and Backstitch, embroider facial detail on F and letters on two A pieces as indicated on graphs.
3: For handle bone, with beige, Whipstitch two J pieces wrong sides together as indicated; Overcast unfinished edges of handle bone and remaining J piece.
4: With sail blue, Whipstitch and assemble A-E pieces and handle bone as indicated and according to Box Assembly Diagram.
5: Glue dog pieces and remaining bone together and to one solid box side as shown in photo.❖

A – Box Side
(cut 4) 32 x 37 holes

C – Box Lip
(cut 1) 32 x 32 holes

Cut Out

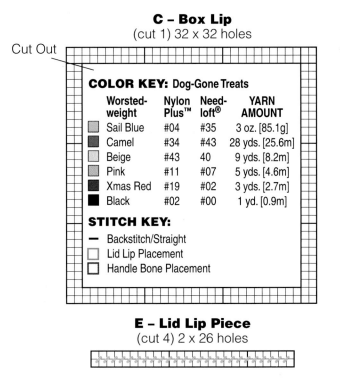

COLOR KEY: Dog-Gone Treats

	Worsted-weight	Nylon Plus™	Need-loft®	YARN AMOUNT
	Sail Blue	#04	#35	3 oz. [85.1g]
	Camel	#34	#43	28 yds. [25.6m]
	Beige	#43	40	9 yds. [8.2m]
	Pink	#11	#07	5 yds. [4.6m]
	Xmas Red	#19	#02	3 yds. [2.7m]
	Black	#02	#00	1 yd. [0.9m]

STITCH KEY:
- — Backstitch/Straight
- ☐ Lid Lip Placement
- ☐ Handle Bone Placement

E – Lid Lip Piece
(cut 4) 2 x 26 holes

Dog-Gone Treats

Instructions and photo on pages 40 & 41

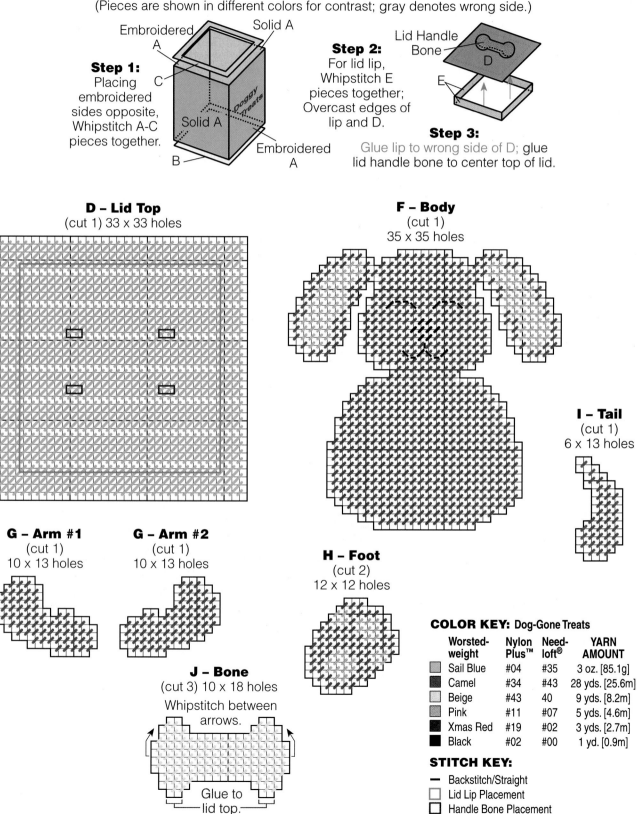

Box Assembly Diagram
(Pieces are shown in different colors for contrast; gray denotes wrong side.)

Embroidered
Solid A
A

Step 1:
Placing
embroidered
sides opposite,
Whipstitch A-C
pieces together.

C
Solid A
Doggy Treats
B
Embroidered
A

Step 2:
For lid lip,
Whipstitch E
pieces together;
Overcast edges of
lip and D.

Lid Handle
Bone
D
E

Step 3:
Glue lip to wrong side of D; glue
lid handle bone to center top of lid.

D – Lid Top
(cut 1) 33 x 33 holes

F – Body
(cut 1)
35 x 35 holes

I – Tail
(cut 1)
6 x 13 holes

G – Arm #1
(cut 1)
10 x 13 holes

G – Arm #2
(cut 1)
10 x 13 holes

H – Foot
(cut 2)
12 x 12 holes

J – Bone
(cut 3) 10 x 18 holes
Whipstitch between
arrows.

Glue to
lid top.

COLOR KEY: Dog-Gone Treats

	Worsted-weight	Nylon Plus™	Need-loft®	YARN AMOUNT
	Sail Blue	#04	#35	3 oz. [85.1g]
	Camel	#34	#43	28 yds. [25.6m]
	Beige	#43	40	9 yds. [8.2m]
	Pink	#11	#07	5 yds. [4.6m]
	Xmas Red	#19	#02	3 yds. [2.7m]
	Black	#02	#00	1 yd. [0.9m]

STITCH KEY:
— Backstitch/Straight
☐ Lid Lip Placement
☐ Handle Bone Placement

INSTRUCTIONS ON
NEXT PAGE

Barn Tissue Cover

Designed by Sandra Miller Maxfield

Barn Tissue Cover

Photo on page 43

SIZE
Loosely covers a boutique-style tissue box.

SKILL LEVEL: Average

MATERIALS
- ❑ 2½ sheets of 7-count plastic canvas
- ❑ Wood excelsior
- ❑ Velcro® closure (optional)
- ❑ Craft glue or glue gun
- ❑ Worsted-weight or plastic canvas yarn; for amounts see Color Key.

CUTTING INSTRUCTIONS
A: For front and back, cut two (one for front and one for back) according to graph.

B: For sides, cut two 32 x 37 holes.

C: For lower roof pieces, cut two 9 x 32 holes.

D: For upper roof pieces, cut two according to graph.

E: For top roof pieces, cut two 4 x 11 holes.

F: For door trim, cut one according to graph.

G: For front window trim, cut one according to graph.

H: For side window trims, cut two according to graph.

I: For cow head, cut one according to graph.

J: For hen, cut one according to graph.

K: For pig, cut one according to graph.

L: For optional bottom and flap, cut one 32 x 32 holes for bottom and one 12 x 32 holes for flap (no graphs).

STITCHING INSTRUCTIONS
NOTE: L pieces are not worked.

1: Using colors and stitches indicated, work one A for front, B-F and I-K pieces according to graphs; omitting window and door stitches and continuing red background pattern across center of piece, work remaining A for back according to graph.

2: With white, Overcast edges of F-H pieces; with colors indicated on graphs and with matching colors, Overcast edges of I-K pieces.

3: Using colors (Separate into individual plies, if desired.) and embroidery stitches indicated, embroider detail on I-K pieces as indicated.

4: With matching colors, Whipstitch A-E and L pieces together as indicated and according to Tissue Cover Assembly Illustration; Overcast unfinished edges. If desired, glue closure to flap and inside of Cover.

5: Glue window trims over windows; glue excelsior to bottom edge of front window, wrong side of cow's muzzle and lower edge of one Cover side (see photo). Glue cow head to front over door trim, hen to front window over excelsior and pig to Cover side over excelsior as shown.✣

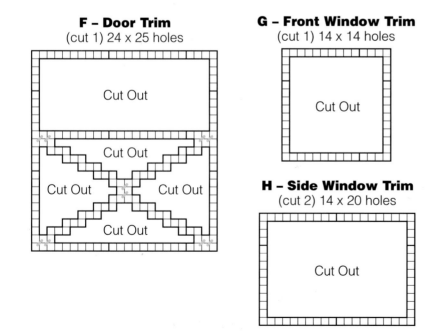

F – Door Trim
(cut 1) 24 x 25 holes

Cut Out

Cut Out

Cut Out Cut Out

Cut Out

G – Front Window Trim
(cut 1) 14 x 14 holes

Cut Out

H – Side Window Trim
(cut 2) 14 x 20 holes

Cut Out

COLOR KEY: Barn Tissue Cover

	Worsted-weight	Nylon Plus™	Need-loft®	YARN AMOUNT
■	Red	#20	#01	3 oz. [85.1g]
☐	Yellow	#26	#57	42 yds. [38.4m]
■	Black	#02	#00	9 yds. [8.2m]
☐	White	#01	#41	8 yds. [7.3m]
☐	Coral	#14	#66	4 yds. [3.7m]
■	Holly	#31	#27	1 yd. [0.9m]
■	Xmas Red	#19	#02	1 yd. [0.9m]
☐	Camel	#34	#43	½ yd. [0.5m]
■	Pink	#11	#07	½ yd. [0.5m]

STITCH KEY:
- — Backstitch/Straight
- ● French Knot

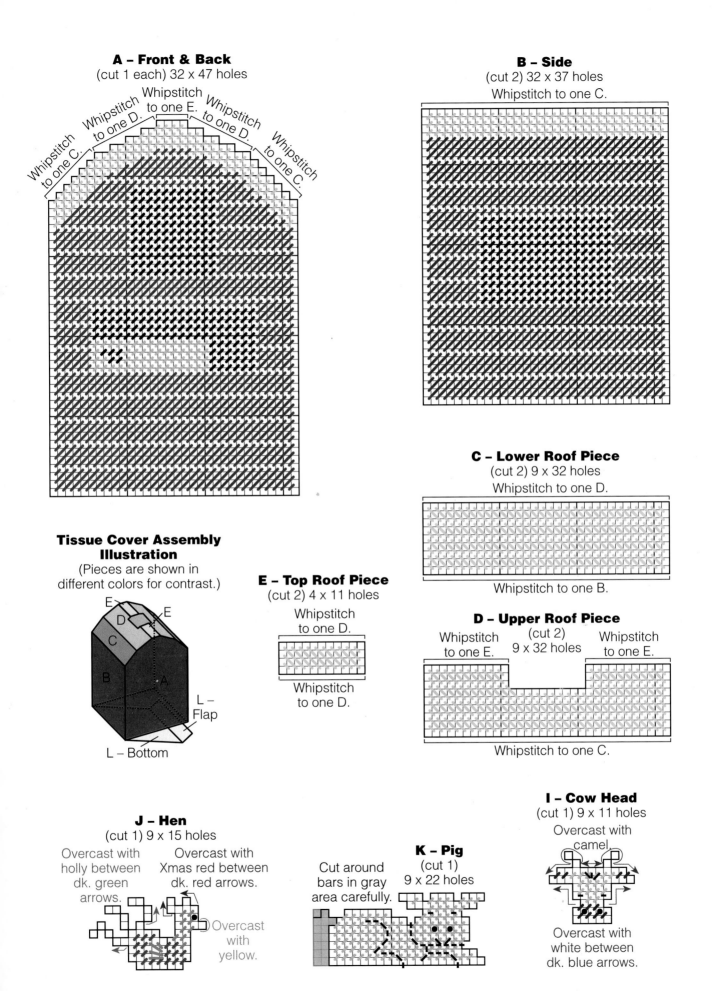

A – Front & Back
(cut 1 each) 32 x 47 holes

Whipstitch to one C.
Whipstitch to one D.
Whipstitch to one E.
Whipstitch to one D.
Whipstitch to one C.

B – Side
(cut 2) 32 x 37 holes
Whipstitch to one C.

C – Lower Roof Piece
(cut 2) 9 x 32 holes
Whipstitch to one D.

Whipstitch to one B.

Tissue Cover Assembly Illustration
(Pieces are shown in different colors for contrast.)

E
E
D
C
B
A
L – Flap
L – Bottom

E – Top Roof Piece
(cut 2) 4 x 11 holes

Whipstitch to one D.

Whipstitch to one D.

D – Upper Roof Piece
(cut 2)
9 x 32 holes

Whipstitch to one E.

Whipstitch to one E.

Whipstitch to one C.

J – Hen
(cut 1) 9 x 15 holes

Overcast with holly between dk. green arrows.

Overcast with Xmas red between dk. red arrows.

Overcast with yellow.

K – Pig
(cut 1)
9 x 22 holes

Cut around bars in gray area carefully.

I – Cow Head
(cut 1) 9 x 11 holes

Overcast with camel.

Overcast with white between dk. blue arrows.

Farm Friends ● 45

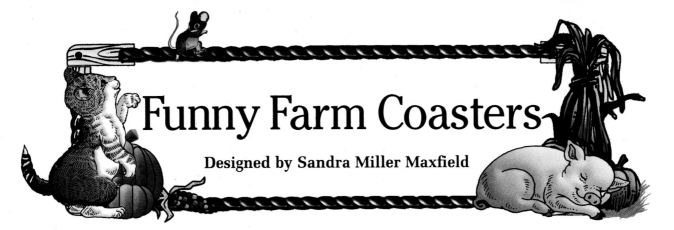

Funny Farm Coasters

Designed by Sandra Miller Maxfield

SIZES
Each Coaster is about 4" x 5" [10.2cm x 12.7cm]; Holder is 2½" x 5¼" x 3⅝" tall [6.4cm x 13.3cm x 9.2cm].

SKILL LEVEL: Average

MATERIALS
❑ Two sheets of 7-count plastic canvas
❑ Worsted-weight or plastic canvas yarn; for amounts see Color Key.

CUTTING INSTRUCTIONS
NOTE: Graphs continued on page 48.
A: For each Coaster, cut one each according to graphs.
B: For Holder sides, cut two according to graph.
C: For Holder ends, cut two according to graph.
D: For Holder bottom, cut one 17 x 33 holes (no graph).

STITCHING INSTRUCTIONS
NOTE: D is not worked.

1: Using colors indicated and Continental Stitch, work A-C pieces according to graphs; omitting attachment edges, with white, Overcast edges of B and C pieces. With Xmas red for topknot on Hilarious Hen, camel for horns on Comic Cow and with matching colors as shown in photo, Overcast edges of A pieces.

2: Using colors (Separate into individual plies, if desired.) and embroidery stitches (Leave 1" [2.5cm] loops on Rya Knots.) indicated, embroider detail on Comic Cow, Droll Ducky and Humorous Horse as indicated on graphs. Leaving 1" [2.5cm] tails, with cinnamon, work a Lark's Head Knot on horse tail as indicated. Clip through Rya Knot loops and fray ends of Rya Knots and Lark's Head Knot to fluff.

3: For Holder, with white, Whipstitch B-D pieces together as indicated and according to Holder Assembly Illustration, Overcasting unfinished edges of bottom as you work. ✽

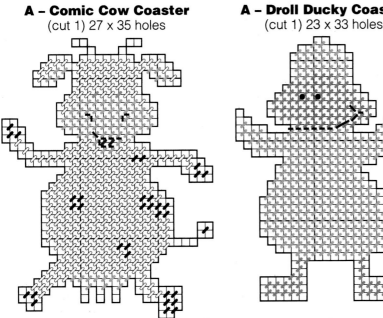

A – Comic Cow Coaster
(cut 1) 27 x 35 holes

A – Droll Ducky Coaster
(cut 1) 23 x 33 holes

COLOR KEY: Funny Farm Coasters

	Worsted-weight	Nylon Plus™	Need-loft®	YARN AMOUNT
▨	White	#01	#41	33 yds. [30.2m]
▓	Camel	#34	#43	9 yds. [8.2m]
■	Black	#02	#00	7 yds. [6.4m]
▨	Lemon	#25	#20	6 yds. [5.5m]
▨	Pink	#11	#07	3 yds. [2.7m]
▨	Tangerine	#15	#11	3 yds. [1.7m]
▨	Pumpkin	#50	#12	2 yds. [1.8m]
■	Cinnamon	#44	#14	1 yd. [0.9m]
▨	Yellow	#26	#57	1 yd. [0.9m]
▨	Bright Blue	–	#60	½ yd. [0.5m]
☐	Xmas Red	#19	#02	½ yd. [0.5m]
■	Lavender	#12	#05	¼ yd. [0.2m]

STITCH KEY:
— Backstitch/Straight
● French Knot
↩ Rya Knot
✦ Lark's Head Knot

Funny Farm Coasters

Instructions and photo on pages 46 & 47

A – Humorous Horse Coaster
(cut 1) 30 x 36 holes

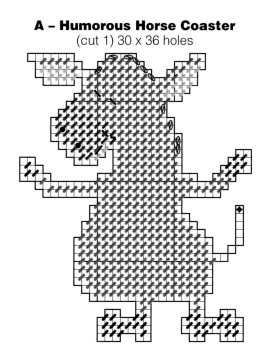

A – Hilarious Hen Coaster
(cut 1) 26 x 35 holes

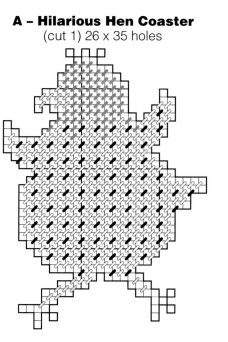

B – Holder Side
(cut 2) 23 x 33 holes

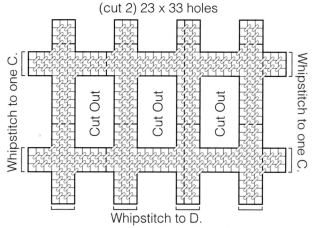

COLOR KEY: Funny Farm Coasters

	Worsted-weight	Nylon Plus™	Need-loft®	YARN AMOUNT
▨	White	#01	#41	33 yds. [30.2m]
▨	Camel	#34	#43	9 yds. [8.2m]
■	Black	#02	#00	7 yds. [6.4m]
▨	Lemon	#25	#20	6 yds. [5.5m]
▨	Pink	#11	#07	3 yds. [2.7m]
▨	Tangerine	#15	#11	3 yds. [1.7m]
▨	Pumpkin	#50	#12	2 yds. [1.8m]
■	Cinnamon	#44	#14	1 yd. [0.9m]
▨	Yellow	#26	#57	1 yd. [0.9m]
▨	Bright Blue	–	#60	1/2 yd. [0.5m]
☐	Xmas Red	#19	#02	1/2 yd. [0.5m]
■	Lavender	#12	#05	1/4 yd. [0.2m]

STITCH KEY:
- — Backstitch/Straight
- ● French Knot
- ⌁ Rya Knot
- ✦ Lark's Head Knot

Holder Assembly Illustration

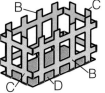

C – Holder End
(cut 2) 17 x 23 holes

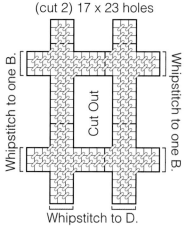

INSTRUCTIONS ON NEXT PAGE

Kitchen Chickens

Designed by Michele Wilcox

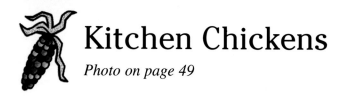

Kitchen Chickens

Photo on page 49

SIZES

Table Runner is 7¼" x 21¼" [18.4cm x 54cm]; Basket is 5" square x 3⅛" tall [12.7cm x 7.9cm], not including handle; Tissue Cover snugly covers a boutique-style tissue box.

SKILL LEVEL: Easy

MATERIALS

- ❑ One 13½" x 22½" [34.3cm x 57.2cm] and two standard-size sheets of 7-count plastic canvas
- ❑ Craft glue or glue gun
- ❑ #5 pearl cotton or six-strand embroidery floss; for amounts see Color Key.
- ❑ Worsted-weight or plastic canvas yarn; for amounts see Color Key.

CUTTING INSTRUCTIONS

A: For Table Runner, cut one from large sheet 48 x 141 holes.
B: For Basket sides, cut four 20 x 32 holes.
C: For Basket bottom, cut one 32 x 32 holes.
D: For Basket handle, cut one 4 x 88 holes (no graph).
E: For Tissue Cover sides, cut four 30 x 36 holes.
F: For Tissue Cover top, cut one according to graph.

STITCHING INSTRUCTIONS

1: Using colors and stitches indicated, work pieces according to graphs and stitch pattern guide; with fern, Overcast edges of A and D pieces and cutout edges of F.
2: Using pearl cotton or six strands floss in colors and embroidery stitches (Wrap twice for all eyes and three times around needle for topknot French Knots on E pieces.) indicated, embroider detail on A, B and E pieces as indicated on graphs.
3: For Basket, holding right side of bottom facing out, with fern, Whipstitch B and C pieces together; with white, Overcast unfinished edges. Glue each end of D to opposite sides on inside of Basket.
4: For Tissue Cover, with fern, Whipstitch E and F pieces together; Overcast unfinished edges.✻

A – Table Runner (cut 1) 48 x 141 holes

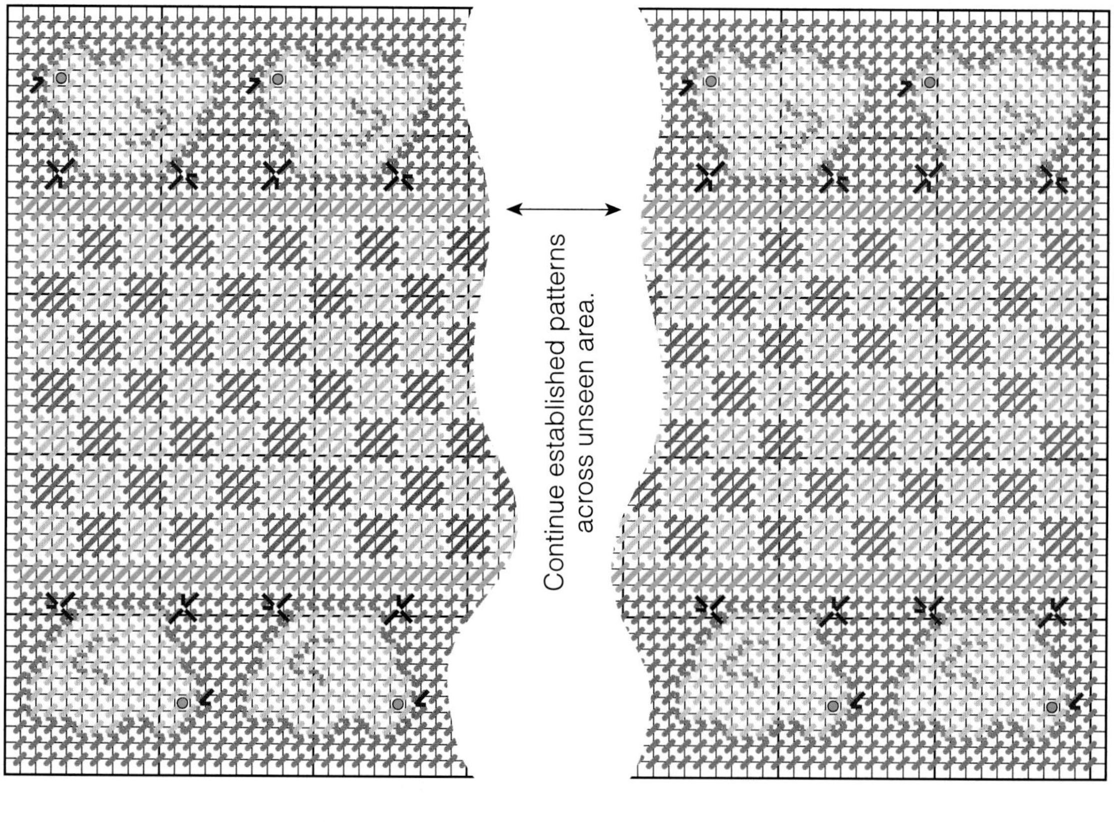
Continue established patterns across unseen area.

B – Basket Side
(cut 4) 20 x 32 holes

C – Basket Bottom
(cut 1) 32 x 32 holes

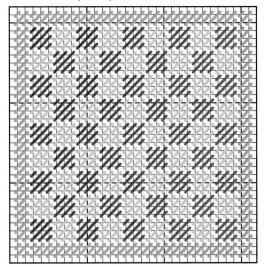

COLOR KEY: Kitchen Chickens

Pearl cotton or floss			AMOUNT
Orange			26 yds. [23.8m]
Red			10 yds. [9.1m]
Blue			3 yds. [2.7m]

Worsted-weight	Nylon Plus™	Need-loft®	YARN AMOUNT
Straw	#41	#19	93 yds. [85m]
White	#01	#41	64 yds. [58.5m]
Fern	#57	#23	58 yds. [53m]
Tangerine	#15	#11	50 yds. [45.7m]
Red	#20	#01	2 yds. [1.8m]

STITCH KEY:

— Backstitch/Straight

● French Knot

Handle Stitch Pattern Guide

Continue established pattern across entire piece.

E – Tissue Cover Side
(cut 4) 30 x 36 holes

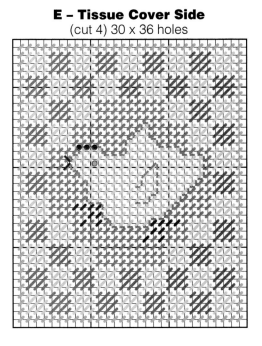

F – Tissue Cover Top
(cut 1) 30 x 30 holes

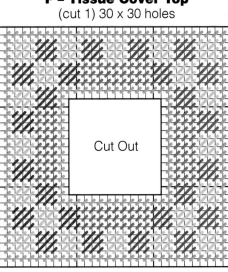

Cut Out

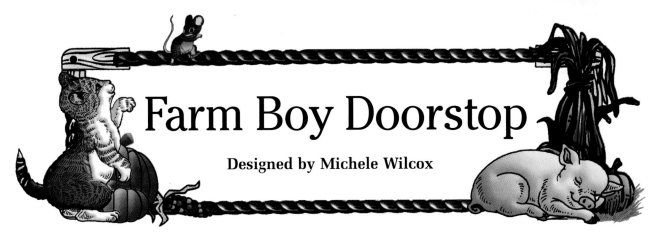

Farm Boy Doorstop

Designed by Michele Wilcox

SIZE
2½" x 4" x 7¾" tall [6.4cm x 10.2cm x 19.7cm], not including farm boy.

SKILL LEVEL: Easy

MATERIALS
- ❑ 1½ sheets of 7-count plastic canvas
- ❑ Two light blue ½" [13mm] buttons
- ❑ Brick or zip-close bag filled with sand, gravel or other weighting material
- ❑ Sewing needle
- ❑ Craft glue or glue gun
- ❑ #5 pearl cotton or six-strand embroidery floss; for amounts see Color Key.
- ❑ Worsted-weight or plastic canvas yarn; for amounts see Color Key.

CUTTING INSTRUCTIONS
NOTE: Graphs continued on page 54.
A: For farm boy, cut one according to graph.
B: For Cover sides, cut two 26 x 51 holes.
C: For Cover ends, cut two 16 x 51 holes.
D: For Cover top and bottom, cut two (one for top and one for bottom) 16 x 26 holes.

STITCHING INSTRUCTIONS
NOTE: One D is not worked for bottom.
1: Using colors and stitches indicated, work A-C pieces and one D piece for top according to graphs; with black for crow and with matching colors, Overcast edges of A.
2: Using pearl cotton or six strands floss and embroidery stitches indicated, embroider detail on A as indicated on graph. With blue pearl cotton or six strands floss, sew buttons to A as indicated.
3: With matching colors, Whipstitch B-D pieces together, inserting weight before closing. Matching bottom edges, glue A to front as shown in photo.✳

COLOR KEY: Farm Boy Doorstop

Pearl cotton or floss			AMOUNT
▨ Green			3 yds. [2.7m]
■ Red			½ yd. [0.5m]
■ Black			½ yd. [0.5m]
▨ Blue			½ yd. [0.5m]

Worsted-weight	Nylon Plus™	Need-loft®	YARN AMOUNT
▨ Sail Blue	#04	#35	46 yds. [42.1m]
▨ Camel	#34	#43	36 yds. [32.9m]
▨ Denim	#06	#33	14 yds. [12.8m]
▨ Cinnamon	#44	#14	8 yds. [7.3m]
▨ White	#01	#41	5 yds. [4.6m]
▨ Beige	#43	#40	4 yds. [3.7m]
▨ Black	#02	#00	2 yds. [1.8m]
▨ Red	#20	#01	2 yds. [1.8m]
▨ Fern	#57	#23	1 yd. [0.9m]
▨ Tangerine	#15	#11	1 yd. [0.9m]

STITCH KEY:
- — Backstitch/Straight
- ● French Knot
- ○ Button Attachment

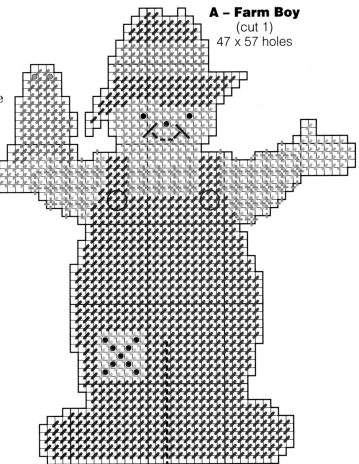

A – Farm Boy
(cut 1)
47 x 57 holes

Farm Boy Doorstop

Instructions and photo on pages 52 & 53

B – Cover Side
(cut 2) 26 x 51 holes

C – Cover End
(cut 2) 16 x 51 holes

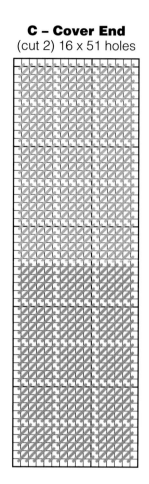

COLOR KEY: Farm Boy Doorstop

Pearl cotton or floss			AMOUNT
▨ Green			3 yds. [2.7m]
■ Red			1/2 yd. [0.5m]
■ Black			1/2 yd. [0.5m]
▨ Blue			1/2 yd. [0.5m]

Worsted-weight	Nylon Plus™	Need-loft®	YARN AMOUNT
▨ Sail Blue	#04	#35	46 yds. [42.1m]
▨ Camel	#34	#43	36 yds. [32.9m]
■ Denim	#06	#33	14 yds. [12.8m]
■ Cinnamon	#44	#14	8 yds. [7.3m]
▨ White	#01	#41	5 yds. [4.6m]
▨ Beige	#43	#40	4 yds. [3.7m]
▨ Black	#02	#00	2 yds. [1.8m]
▨ Red	#20	#01	2 yds. [1.8m]
▨ Fern	#57	#23	1 yd. [0.9m]
▨ Tangerine	#15	#11	1 yd. [0.9m]

D – Cover Top & Bottom
(cut 1 each) 16 x 26 holes

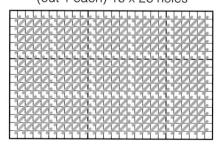

STITCH KEY:
— Backstitch/Straight
● French Knot
○ Button Attachment

54 ● *Farm Friends*

INSTRUCTIONS
ON NEXT PAGE

Swimming in the Rain

Designed by Michele Wilcox

Swimming in the Rain

Photo on page 55

SIZES

Screen is 26" open x 12⅛" tall
[66cm x 30.8cm].

SKILL LEVEL: Easy

MATERIALS

❑ Three sheets of 5-count plastic canvas
❑ #3 pearl cotton or six-strand embroidery floss; for amounts see Color Key.
❑ Worsted-weight or plastic canvas yarn; for amounts see Color Key.

CUTTING INSTRUCTIONS

A: For Screen end sections #1 and #2, cut one each from 5-count 44 x 60 holes.

B: For Screen center section, cut one from 5-count 40 x 60 holes.

STITCHING INSTRUCTIONS

NOTES: Use a double strand for stitching and a single strand of yarn for embroidery.

1: Using colors and stitches indicated, work pieces according to graphs; fill in uncoded areas using baby blue and Continental Stitch.
2: Using yarn and pearl cotton or six strands floss in colors and embroidery stitches indicated, embroider detail on pieces as indicated on graphs.
3: For Screen, with matching colors, Whip pieces together as indicated; Overcast unfinished edges.�֍

A – Screen End Section #1
(cut 1 from 5-count) 44 x 60 holes

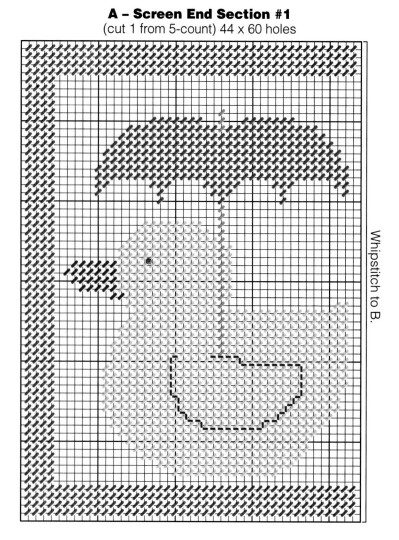

Whipstitch to B.

COLOR KEY: Swimming in the Rain

Pearl cotton or floss			AMOUNT
▨ Teal			1 yd. [0.9m]

Worsted-weight	Nylon Plus™	Need-loft®	YARN AMOUNT
☐ Baby Blue	#05	#36	3½ oz. [99.2g]
☐ Straw	#41	#19	2 oz. [56.7g]
▨ Watermelon	#54	#55	56 yds. [51.2m]
▨ Teal Blue	#08	#50	38 yds. [34.7m]
▨ Pumpkin	#50	#12	6 yds. [5.5m]
▨ Cinnamon	#44	#14	5 yds. [4.6m]

STITCH KEY:

— Backstitch/Straight
● French Knot

B – Screen Center Section
(cut 1 from 5-count) 40 x 60 holes

A – Screen End Section #2
(cut 1 from 5-count) 44 x 60 holes

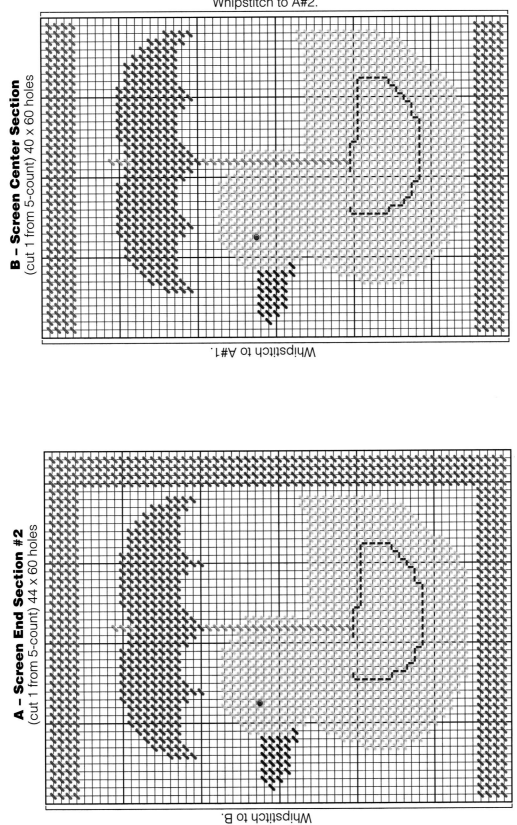

Whipstitch to A#1.

Whipstitch to B.

Garden Sunshine

Steal a little of Mother Nature's glory for yourself! Glistening wings and sparkling colors await you in this enchanted realm that blends fantasy and reality. Whimsical designs aglow with sunny hues spread a ray of happiness for all to behold. You'll bask in the warmth of satisfaction at the bounty of beautiful designs you can stitch for home, holiday and fashion. Sunflowers, honey bees and trailing blooms will soothe your senses as they pacify your spirit with the serenity and repose only gardens can provide. Kick off your shoes, wiggle your toes and rest assured you're in for a delightful stitching adventure.

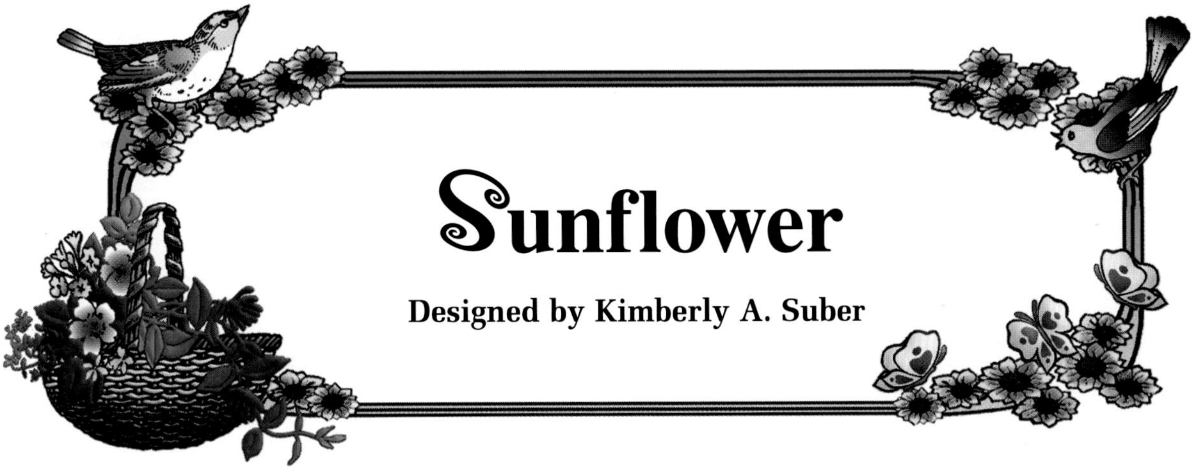

Sunflower

Designed by Kimberly A. Suber

SIZE

6" x 9" [15.2cm x 22.9cm], not including hanger.

SKILL LEVEL: Easy

MATERIALS

- ❑ One sheet of 7-count plastic canvas
- ❑ ½ yd. [0.5m] of natural raffia
- ❑ ⅓ yd. [0.3m] of blue ⅜" [10mm] satin ribbon
- ❑ Craft glue or glue gun
- ❑ Worsted-weight or plastic canvas yarn; for amounts see Color Key.

CUTTING INSTRUCTIONS

A: For Sunflower Motif, cut one 40 x 60 holes.

B: For button, cut one according to graph.

STITCHING INSTRUCTIONS

1: Using colors and stitches indicated, work pieces according to graphs. With royal for motif and tangerine for button, Overcast edges.

2: With black and Cross Stitch, embroider detail on B as indicated on graph.

NOTE: Tie raffia into a bow.

3: Glue ends of ribbon to wrong side of A as indicated; glue raffia and button to center of ribbon as shown in photo.✻

COLOR KEY: Sunflower

Worsted-weight	Nylon Plus™	Need-loft®	YARN AMOUNT
Sail Blue	#04	#35	10 yds. [9.1m]
White	#01	#41	8 yds. [7.3m]
Royal	#09	#32	7 yds. [6.4m]
Crimson	#53	#42	5 yds. [4.6m]
Tangerine	#15	#11	4 yds. [3.7m]
Xmas Green	#58	#28	3 yds. [2.7m]
Cinnamon	#44	#14	2 yds. [1.8m]
Black	#02	#00	1/2 yd. [0.5m]

STITCH KEY:

- × Cross Stitch
- ✦ Ribbon Placement

B – Button
(cut 1)
6 x 6 holes

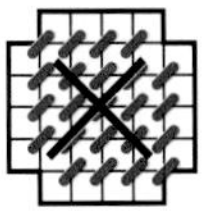

A – Sunflower Motif
(cut 1) 40 x 60 holes

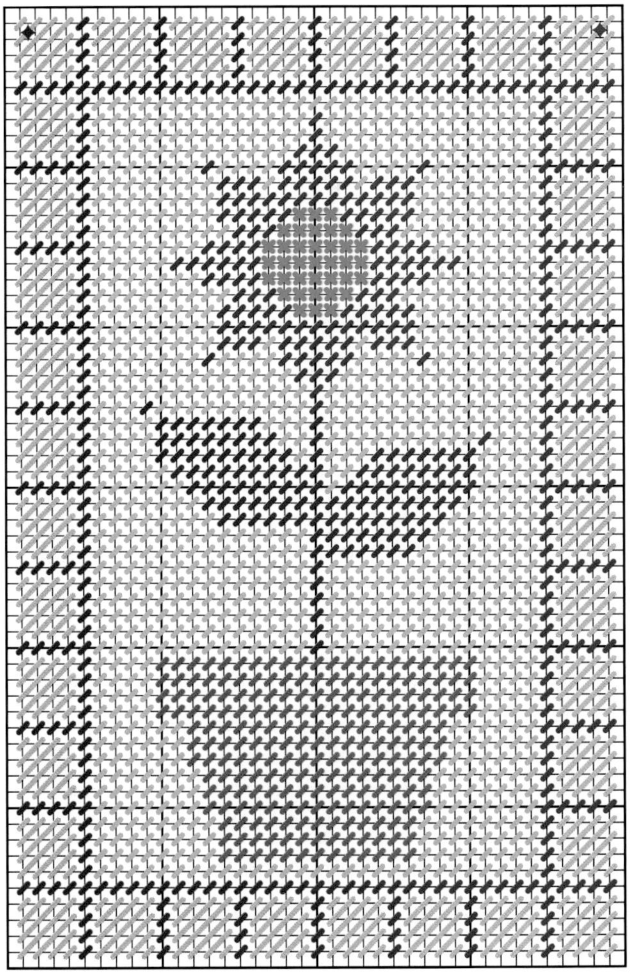

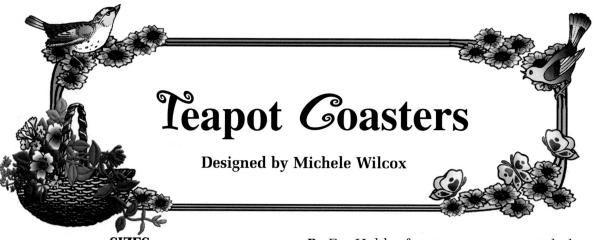

Ladybug Cover

Designed by Michele Wilcox

SIZE

Snugly covers a boutique-style tissue box.

SKILL LEVEL: Easy

MATERIALS

- ❑ 1½ sheets of 7-count plastic canvas
- ❑ #5 pearl cotton or six-strand embroidery floss; for amount see Color Key on page 64.
- ❑ Worsted-weight or plastic canvas yarn; for amounts see Color Key.

CUTTING INSTRUCTIONS

NOTE: Graphs on page 64.
A: For sides #1, cut two 30 x 36 holes.
B: For sides #2, cut two 30 x 36 holes.
C: For top, cut one according to graph.

STITCHING INSTRUCTIONS

1: Using colors and stitches indicated, work pieces according to graphs; fill in uncoded areas of A and B pieces using white and Continental Stitch. With white, Overcast cutout edges of C.
2: Using pearl cotton or six strands floss and embroidery stitches indicated, embroider detail on A and B pieces as indicated on graphs.
3: Alternating A and B pieces, with white, Whipstitch A-C pieces wrong sides together, forming Cover; Overcast unfinished edges.❇

Teapot Coasters

Designed by Michele Wilcox

SIZES

Each Coaster is 4" square [10.2cm]; Holder is 2" x 4⅜" x 2¼" tall [5.1cm x 11.1cm x 5.7cm].

SKILL LEVEL: Easy

MATERIALS

- ❑ One sheet of 7-count plastic canvas
- ❑ #5 pearl cotton or six-strand embroidery floss; for amount see Color Key on page 65.
- ❑ Worsted-weight or plastic canvas yarn; for amounts see Color Key.

CUTTING INSTRUCTIONS

NOTE: Graphs on page 65.
A: For Coasters, cut four 26 x 26 holes.
B: For Holder front, cut one 14 x 28 holes.
C: For Holder back, cut one 14 x 28 holes.
D: For Holder ends, cut two 12 x 14 holes.
E: For Holder bottom, cut one 12 x 28 holes.

STITCHING INSTRUCTIONS

1: Using colors and stitches indicated, work pieces according to graphs; with matching colors as shown in photo, Overcast edges of A pieces.
2: Using pearl cotton or six strands floss and Backstitch, embroider detail on B as indicated on graph.
3: For Holder, with sail blue, Whipstitch B-E pieces wrong sides together; Overcast unfinished edges.❇

Ladybug Cover

Instructions and photo on pages 62 & 63

A – Side #1
(cut 2)
30 x 36 holes

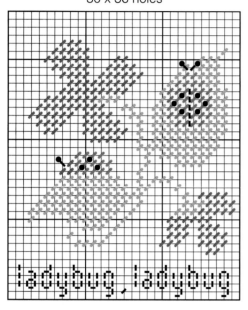

COLOR KEY: Ladybug Cover

	#5 pearl cotton or floss			AMOUNT
■	Black			10 yds. [9.1m]

	Worsted-weight	Nylon Plus™	Need-loft®	YARN AMOUNT
	White	#01	#41	55 yds. [50.3m]
	Xmas Green	#58	#28	18 yds. [16.5m]
	Tangerine	#15	#11	13 yds. [11.9m]
	Red	#20	#01	8 yds. [7.3m]
	Black	#02	#00	4 yds. [3.7m]
	Cinnamon	#44	#14	2 yds. [1.8m]

STITCH KEY:
— Backstitch/Straight
● French Knot

B – Side #2
(cut 2)
30 x 36 holes

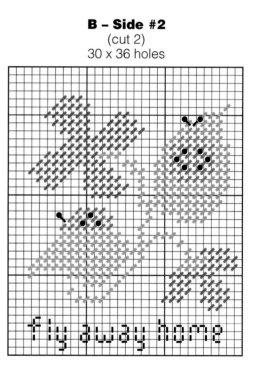

C – Top
(cut 1)
30 x 30 holes

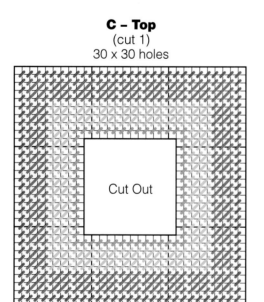

Teapot Coasters

Instructions and photo on pages 62 & 63

A – Coaster
(cut 4) 26 x 26 holes

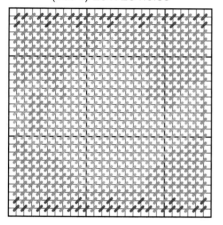

COLOR KEY: Teapot Coasters

#5 pearl cotton or floss			AMOUNT
■ Black			2 yds. [1.8m]

Worsted-weight	Nylon Plus™	Need-loft®	YARN AMOUNT
☐ Sail Blue	#04	#35	30 yds. [27.4m]
☐ Yellow	#26	#57	25 yds. [22.9m]
☐ White	#01	#41	12 yds. [11m]
■ Xmas Green	#58	#28	1 yd. [0.9m]

STITCH KEY:

— Backstitch/Straight

B – Holder Front
(cut 1) 14 x 28 holes

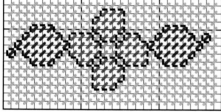

C – Holder Back
(cut 1) 14 x 28 holes

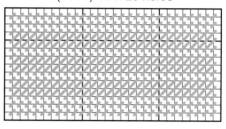

E – Holder Bottom
(cut 1) 12 x 28 holes

D – Holder End
(cut 2)
12 x 14 holes

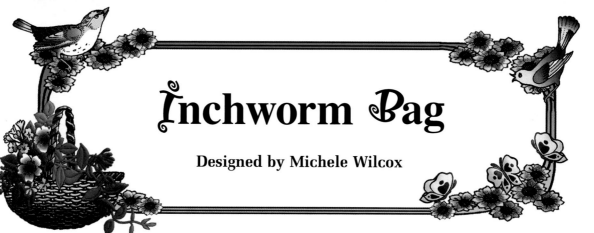

Inchworm Bag

Designed by Michele Wilcox

SIZE
3½" x 7" x 6½" tall [8.9cm x 17.8cm x 16.5cm], not including handles.

SKILL LEVEL: Easy

MATERIALS
- ❑ Two sheets of 7-count plastic canvas
- ❑ Craft glue or glue gun
- ❑ #5 pearl cotton or six-strand embroidery floss; for amounts see Color Key.
- ❑ Worsted-weight or plastic canvas yarn; for amounts see Color Key.

CUTTING INSTRUCTIONS
A: For front and back, cut two (one for front and one for back) 43 x 46 holes.

B: For sides, cut two 22 x 43 holes (no graph).

C: For bottom, cut one 22 x 46 holes (no graph).

D: For handles, cut two 4 x 88 holes (no graph).

STITCHING INSTRUCTIONS
1: Using colors and stitches indicated, work A pieces according to graph; fill in uncoded areas using eggshell and Continental Stitch. Work B and C pieces according to Side and Bottom Stitch Pattern Guide; using yellow and Scotch Stitch over three bars, work D across length of each piece. Overcast edges of D pieces.

2: Using pearl cotton or floss in colors and embroidery stitches indicated, embroider detail on A pieces as indicated on graph.

3: With yellow, Whipstitch A–C pieces wrong sides together, forming Bag; Overcast unfinished edges.

4: Glue handle ends to front and back of Bag as shown in photo.✣

COLOR KEY: Inchworm Bag

#5 pearl cotton or floss		AMOUNT
■ Black		5 yds. [4.6m]
■ Green		4 yds. [3.7m]
■ Red		¼ yd. [.2m]

Worsted-weight	Nylon Plus™	Need-loft®	YARN AMOUNT
▨ Yellow	#26	#57	84 yds. [76.8m]
☐ Eggshell	#24	#39	22 yds. [20.1m]
▨ Fern	#57	#23	4 yds. [3.7m]
▨ Cinnamon	#44	#14	3 yds. [2.7m]
▨ Xmas Green	#58	#28	3 yds. [2.7m]
■ Red	#20	#01	2 yds. [1.8m]
■ Tangerine	#15	#11	1 yd. [0.9m]

STITCH KEY:
- — Backstitch/Straight
- • French Knot

A – Bag Front & Back
(cut 1 each) 43 x 46 holes

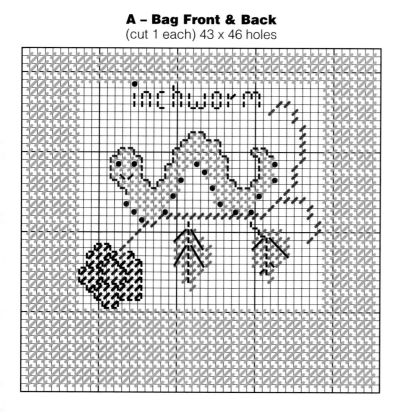

Side & Bottom Stitch Pattern Guide

Continue established pattern up and across each entire piece.

Thank You Sampler

Designed by Michele Wilcox

thank you for the
world so sweet

abcdefghijklmnopqrstu
vwxyz
1234567890

SIZE
8¾" x 10½" [22.2cm x 26.7cm].

SKILL LEVEL: Easy

MATERIALS
❑ One sheet of 7-count plastic canvas
❑ #5 pearl cotton or six-strand embroidery floss; for amount see Color Key.
❑ Worsted-weight or plastic canvas yarn; for amounts see Color Key.

CUTTING INSTRUCTIONS
For Sampler, cut one 58 x 70 holes.

STITCHING INSTRUCTIONS
1: Using colors and stitches indicated, work piece according to graph; fill in uncoded area using eggshell and Continental Stitch. With bittersweet, Overcast edges.

2: Using pearl cotton or six strands floss and embroidery stitches indicated, embroider detail on piece as indicated on graph.

3: Hang or display as desired.✣

COLOR KEY: Thank You Sampler

#5 pearl cotton or floss			AMOUNT
■ Black			5 yds. [4.6m]

Worsted-weight	Nylon Plus™	Need-loft®	YARN AMOUNT
☐ Eggshell	#24	#39	35 yds. [32m]
▨ Yellow	#26	#57	14 yds. [12.8m]
▨ Fern	#57	#23	12 yds. [11m]
■ Bittersweet	#18	#52	7 yds. [6.4m]
▨ Xmas Green	#58	#28	4 yds. [3.7m]
■ Crimson	#53	#42	3 yds. [2.7m]
■ Denim	#06	#33	3 yds. [2.7m]
▨ Gold	#27	#17	3 yds. [2.7m]
▨ Black	#02	#00	2 yds. [1.8m]

STITCH KEY:
— Backstitch/Straight
● French Knot

Sampler
(cut 1) 58 x 70 holes

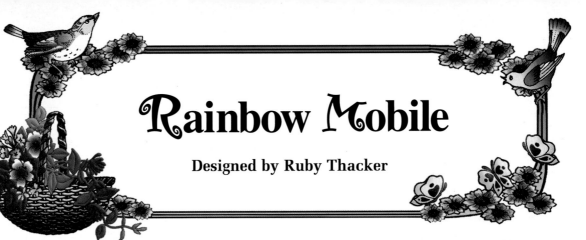

Rainbow Mobile

Designed by Ruby Thacker

SIZE

4½" x 9¼" [11.4cm x 23.5cm], not including hearts.

SKILL LEVEL: Average

MATERIALS

- ❏ One sheet of 7-count plastic canvas
- ❏ 9" [22.9cm] Uniek® plastic canvas radial circle
- ❏ Craft glue or glue gun
- ❏ Sewing needle and gold metallic thread
- ❏ Worsted-weight or plastic canvas yarn; for amounts see Color Key.

CUTTING INSTRUCTIONS

A: For Rainbow pieces, cut two from circle according to graph on page 72.
B: For large hearts, cut eight according to graph.
C: For open hearts, cut six according to graph.
D: For small hearts, cut fourteen according to graph.

STITCHING INSTRUCTIONS

1: Using colors and stitches indicated, work A pieces according to graph. Using Xmas red, royal, fern, purple and Continental Stitch, work two B pieces in each color; work four D in royal and two of each remaining D in Xmas red, bright orange, fern, lemon and purple.
2: For large hearts (make four), with matching colors, Whipstitch two matching color B pieces wrong sides together; for small hearts (make seven), with matching colors, Whipstitch two matching color D pieces wrong sides together.
3: For open hearts (make three), with bright orange, fern and lemon, Whipstitch cut-outs and outer edges of two C pieces together in each color.
NOTES: Cut two 13" [33cm] and four 9" [22.9cm] lengths of metallic thread. For each strand, hold two same-length strings together and knot together at one end.
4: Whipstitch and assemble A pieces, hearts and metallic strands according to Rainbow Mobile Assembly Diagram on page 72.
5: Hang as desired.�

B – Large Heart
(cut 8)
11 x 13 holes

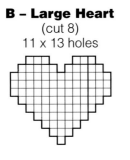

C – Open Heart
(cut 6)
11 x 13 holes

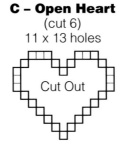

Cut Out

D – Small Heart
(cut 14)
7 x 9 holes

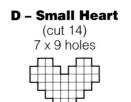

COLOR KEY: Rainbow Mobile

Worsted-weight	Nylon Plus™	Need-loft®	YARN AMOUNT
■ Xmas Red	#19	#02	16 yds. [14.6m]
▨ Bright Orange	#17	#58	13 yds. [11.9m]
▨ Fern	#57	#23	13 yds. [11.9m]
■ Lemon	#25	#20	13 yds. [11.9m]
■ Purple	#21	#46	13 yds. [11.9m]
▨ Royal	#09	#32	13 yds. [11.9m]

STITCH KEY:
✦ String Placement

Rainbow Mobile

Instructions and photo on pages 70 & 71

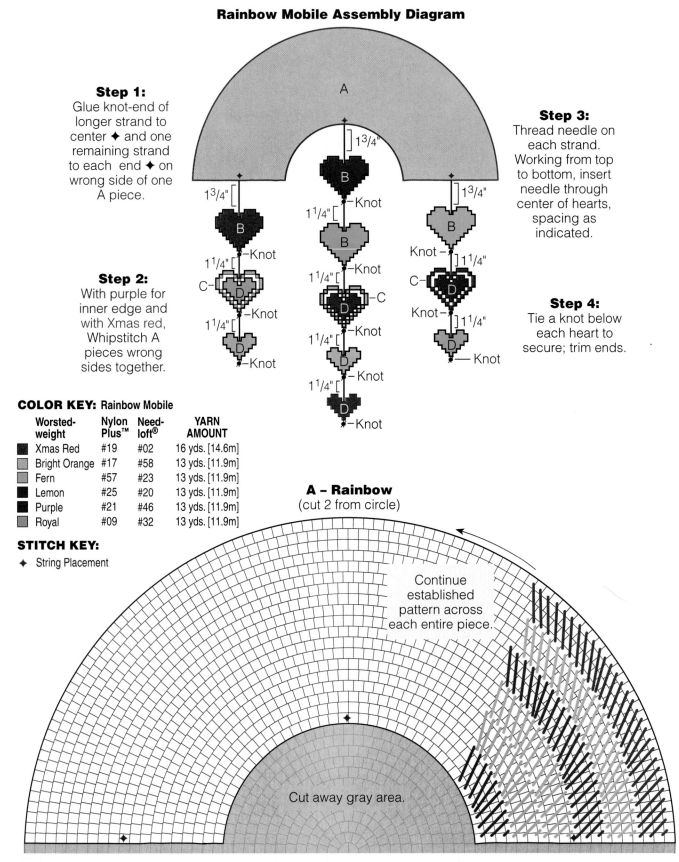

Rainbow Mobile Assembly Diagram

A

1³/₄"

B

B — Knot

1³/₄"

1¹/₄"

B

B — Knot

Step 1:
Glue knot-end of longer strand to center ✦ and one remaining strand to each end ✦ on wrong side of one A piece.

1³/₄"

B — Knot

Step 3:
Thread needle on each strand. Working from top to bottom, insert needle through center of hearts, spacing as indicated.

1¹/₄"

Knot —

1¹/₄"

C—D — Knot

C—D

Knot — D

Step 2:
With purple for inner edge and with Xmas red, Whipstitch A pieces wrong sides together.

1¹/₄"

D — Knot

1¹/₄"

D —C

1¹/₄"

Knot — D

Step 4:
Tie a knot below each heart to secure; trim ends.

1¹/₄"

D — Knot

1¹/₄"

D — Knot

D — Knot

COLOR KEY: Rainbow Mobile

Worsted-weight	Nylon Plus™	Need-loft®	YARN AMOUNT
Xmas Red	#19	#02	16 yds. [14.6m]
Bright Orange	#17	#58	13 yds. [11.9m]
Fern	#57	#23	13 yds. [11.9m]
Lemon	#25	#20	13 yds. [11.9m]
Purple	#21	#46	13 yds. [11.9m]
Royal	#09	#32	13 yds. [11.9m]

STITCH KEY:

✦ String Placement

A – Rainbow
(cut 2 from circle)

Continue established pattern across each entire piece.

Cut away gray area.

Ferris Wheel Planter

Designed by Dawn Austin

INSTRUCTIONS ON
NEXT PAGE

Ferris Wheel Planter

Photo on page 73

SIZE

3½" x 10½" x 10½" tall [8.9cm x 26.7cm x 26.7cm], not including pot rings; holds eight 2"-across x 2½ tall [5.1cm x 6.4cm] clay pots.

SKILL LEVEL: Challenging

MATERIALS

- ❑ Five sheets of 7-count plastic canvas
- ❑ Sixteen Uniek® 3" [7.6cm] plastic canvas radial circles
- ❑ Eight 18" [45.7cm] lengths of 18-gauge wire
- ❑ Craft glue or glue gun
- ❑ Six-strand embroidery floss; for amounts see Color Key on page 20.
- ❑ Worsted-weight or plastic canvas yarn; for amounts see Color Key.

CUTTING INSTRUCTIONS

A: For wheel side pieces, cut four according to graph.

B: For wheel axle, cut one 20 x 33 holes.

C: For pot ring pieces, cut one from each circle according to graph.

STITCHING INSTRUCTIONS

1: Using lavender and Reversed Continental Stitch, work A pieces. Using burgundy and stitches indicated and omitting stitches in overlap area, work B according to graph; overlapping ends as indicated on graph, work remaining stitches in overlap areas through both thicknesses as one to join according to graph.

2: With burgundy, Overcast edges of B. Using six strands floss in colors and embroidery stitches indicated, embroider detail on two A pieces as indicated, forming outer wheel sides; omitting center embroidery, embroider detail on remaining A pieces as indicated, forming inner wheel sides.

NOTE: Cut eight 8" [20.3cm] lengths of wire.

3: Whipstitch and assemble wire and A pieces as indicated and according to Wheel Assembly Diagram. Glue one end of B to center of each inner wheel side, forming ferris wheel.

4: For each pot ring (make 8), using burgundy and stitches indicated, hold two C pieces together and work through both thicknesses as one according to graph; Whipstitch cutout and outer edges together.

5: Glue edges of one pot ring to each set of matching areas on inner sides of ferris wheel as indicated (see photo).✻

C – Pot Ring Piece
(cut 1 from each circle)

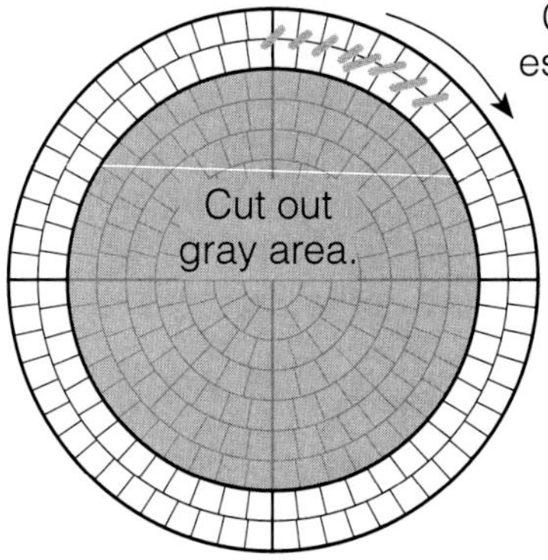

Cut out gray area.
Continue established pattern around entire piece.

Wheel Assembly Diagram
(Pieces are shown in different colors for contrast; gray denotes wrong side.)

Step 1:
Holding one of each inner and outer wheel sides wrong sides together with four 8" wires between, Whipstitch cutout edges together.

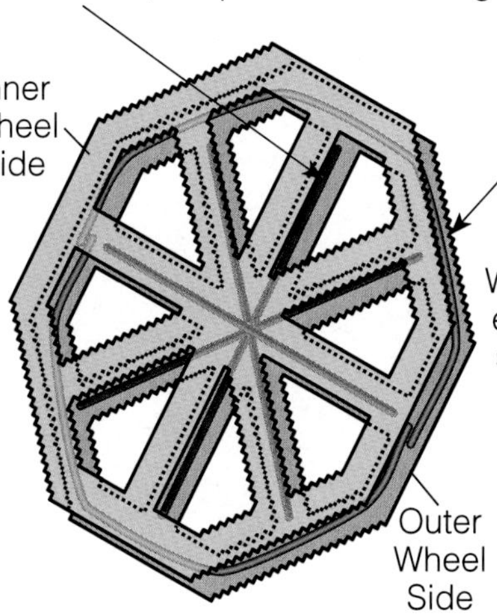

Inner Wheel Side
Outer Wheel Side

Step 2:
Bend two 18" wires to fit around outer solid area of wheel; Whipstitch outer edges of wheel sides together, inserting bent wires before closing.

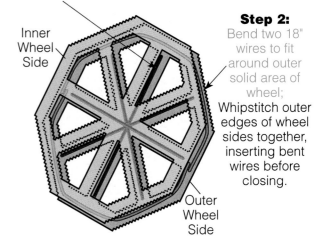

A – Wheel Side Piece (cut 4) 70 x 70 holes

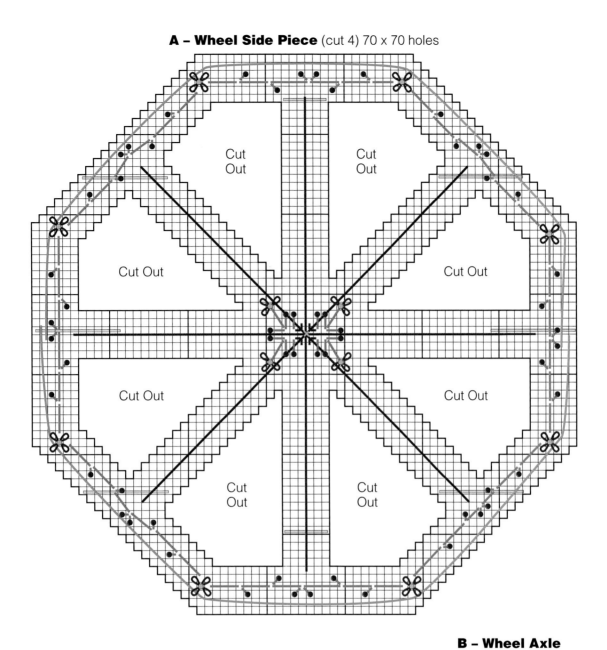

Cut Out

COLOR KEY: Ferris Wheel

Embroidery floss			AMOUNT
■ Green			16 yds. [14.6m]
■ Dk. Red			10 yds. [9.1m]
■ Yellow			5 yds. [4.6m]

Worsted-weight	Nylon Plus™	Need-loft®	YARN AMOUNT
□ Lavender	#12	#05	4 oz. [113.4g]
▨ Burgundy	#13	#03	80 yds. [73.1m]

STITCH KEY:
- ── Backstitch/Straight
- ● French Knot
- ✕ Cross
- ◠ Lazy Daisy
- ── 8" Wire Placement
- ── 18" Wire Placement
- ▭ Pot Ring Placement

B – Wheel Axle
(cut 1) 20 x 33 holes

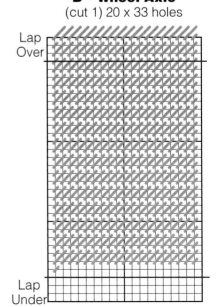

Lap Over

Lap Under

Place Mat

Designed by Michele Wilcox

SIZE
10½" x 13½" [26.7cm x 34.3cm].

SKILL LEVEL: Easy

MATERIALS
- ❑ One sheet of 7-count plastic canvas
- ❑ #5 pearl cotton or six-strand embroidery floss; for amounts see Color Key.
- ❑ Worsted-weight or plastic canvas yarn; for amounts see Color Key.

CUTTING INSTRUCTIONS
For Place Mat, cut one 69 x 89 holes (graph on page 78).

STITCHING INSTRUCTIONS
1: Using colors and stitches indicated, work piece according to graph; with Xmas green, Overcast edges.

2: Using pearl cotton or six strands floss in colors and embroidery stitches indicated, embroider detail on piece as indicated on graph.✣

COLOR KEY: Place Mat

#5 pearl cotton or floss			AMOUNT
■ Black			10 yds. [9.1m]
■ Blue			¼ yd. [0.2m]

Worsted-weight	Nylon Plus™	Need-loft®	YARN AMOUNT
▨ Eggshell	#24	#39	26 yds. [23.8m]
■ Yellow	#26	#57	18 yds. [16.5m]
■ Pumpkin	#50	#12	16 yds. [14.6m]
■ Xmas Green	#58	#28	15 yds. [13.7m]
■ White	#01	#41	11 yds. [10.1m]
■ Bittersweet	#18	#52	9 yds. [8.2m]
■ Mermaid Green	#37	#53	9 yds. [8.2m]
■ Black	#02	#00	2 yds. [1.8m]

STITCH KEY:

- — Backstitch/Straight
- • French Knot

Place Mat

Instructions and photo on pages 76 & 77

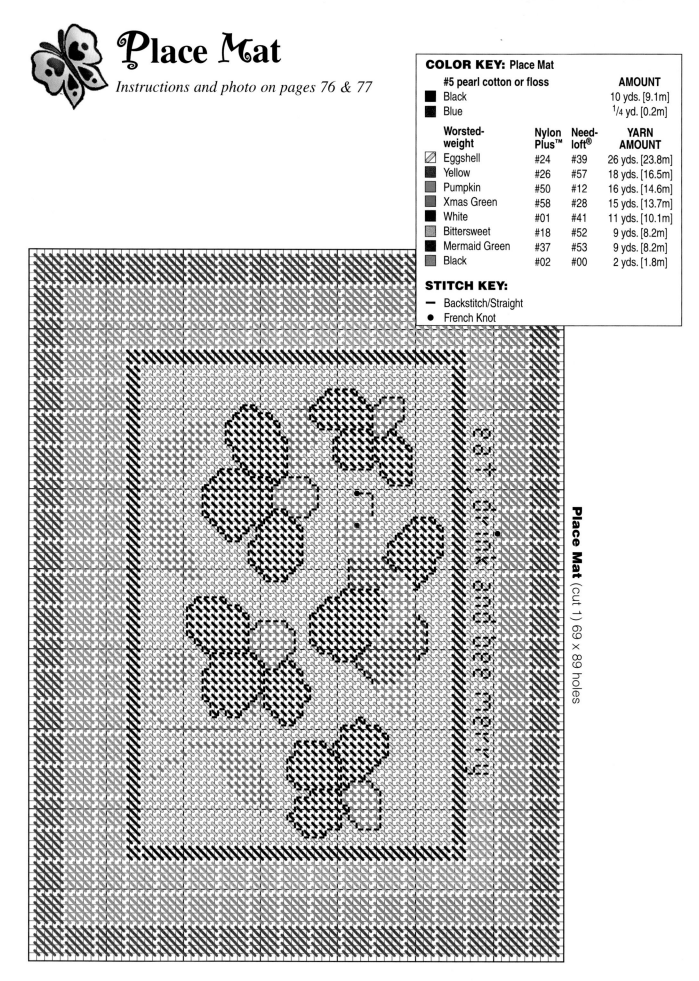

COLOR KEY: Place Mat

#5 pearl cotton or floss			AMOUNT
■ Black			10 yds. [9.1m]
■ Blue			1/4 yd. [0.2m]

Worsted-weight	Nylon Plus™	Need-loft®	YARN AMOUNT
▨ Eggshell	#24	#39	26 yds. [23.8m]
▨ Yellow	#26	#57	18 yds. [16.5m]
▨ Pumpkin	#50	#12	16 yds. [14.6m]
▨ Xmas Green	#58	#28	15 yds. [13.7m]
■ White	#01	#41	11 yds. [10.1m]
▨ Bittersweet	#18	#52	9 yds. [8.2m]
■ Mermaid Green	#37	#53	9 yds. [8.2m]
▨ Black	#02	#00	2 yds. [1.8m]

STITCH KEY:

— Backstitch/Straight

• French Knot

Place Mat (cut 1) 69 x 89 holes

INSTRUCTIONS ON NEXT PAGE

Floral Motif

Designed by Michele Wilcox

Floral Motif

Photo on page 79

SIZE
8¾" x 18⅝" [22.2cm x 47.3cm].

SKILL LEVEL: Easy

MATERIALS
- ❏ Two 13½" x 22½" [34.3cm x 57.2cm] sheets of 7-count plastic canvas
- ❏ #3 and #5 pearl cotton or six-strand embroidery floss; for amounts see Color Key.
- ❏ Worsted-weight or plastic canvas yarn; for amounts see Color Key.

CUTTING INSTRUCTIONS
For Motif, cut two (one for front and one for backing) according to graph.

STITCHING INSTRUCTIONS
NOTE: One piece is not worked for backing.
1: Using colors and stitches indicated, work one piece for front according to graph; fill in uncoded areas of front using eggshell and Continental Stitch.
2: Using pearl cotton or floss in colors and embroidery stitches indicated, embroider detail on front as indicated on graph.
3: Holding backing to wrong side of front, with eggshell, Whipstitch together.
4: Display as desired.✽

Stitching Secret

Don't let needle threading stop you from enjoying plastic canvas needlepoint. There is a very simple tool – a needle threader – that makes the job of threading yarn through the eye of the needle too easy to believe! Many types of needle threaders are available at sewing, fabric, craft and discount stores.

One way to inspire young children to stitch is to help them make their own needle threader. Once needle threading is mastered, children can enjoy hours of needle-crafting fun, and then say, "I made it myself!"

PAPER NEEDLE THREADER:

1. Cut a ⅜" x 2" strip of paper.

2. Fold paper in half.

3. Test size by sliding folded paper through eye of needle. If it does not fit, trim excess paper.

4. Place end of yarn between paper at fold.

5. Insert ends of paper in eye of needle.

6. Pull paper and yarn through gently.

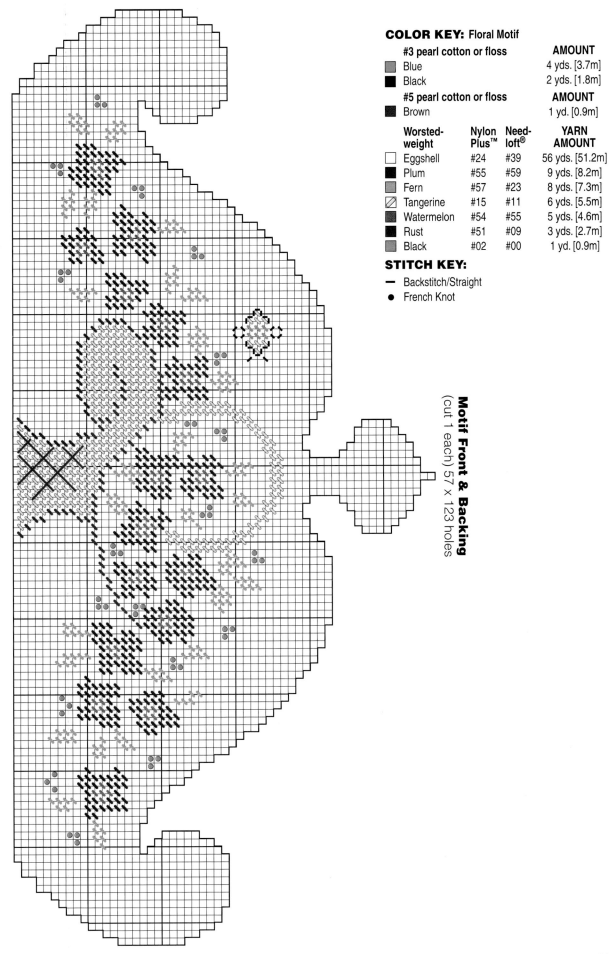

COLOR KEY: Floral Motif

#3 pearl cotton or floss			AMOUNT
▨ Blue			4 yds. [3.7m]
■ Black			2 yds. [1.8m]

#5 pearl cotton or floss			AMOUNT
▨ Brown			1 yd. [0.9m]

Worsted-weight	Nylon Plus™	Need-loft®	YARN AMOUNT
☐ Eggshell	#24	#39	56 yds. [51.2m]
■ Plum	#55	#59	9 yds. [8.2m]
▨ Fern	#57	#23	8 yds. [7.3m]
▨ Tangerine	#15	#11	6 yds. [5.5m]
▨ Watermelon	#54	#55	5 yds. [4.6m]
■ Rust	#51	#09	3 yds. [2.7m]
▨ Black	#02	#00	1 yd. [0.9m]

STITCH KEY:

— Backstitch/Straight

● French Knot

Motif Front & Backing
(cut 1 each) 57 x 123 holes

Summertime Clutch

Designed by Michele Wilcox

SIZE
2¼" x 7⅛" x 4⅜" [5.7cm x 18.1cm x 11.1cm].

SKILL LEVEL: Average

MATERIALS
- ❏ Small plastic canvas purse form
- ❏ One gold purse clasp
- ❏ #3 pearl cotton or six-strand embroidery floss; for amount see Color Key.
- ❏ Worsted-weight or plastic canvas yarn; for amounts see Color Key.

CUTTING INSTRUCTIONS
For Purse, use small purse form.

STITCHING INSTRUCTIONS
1: Using colors and stitches indicated, work piece according to graph. Using pearl cotton or six strands floss and embroidery stitches indicated, embroider detail on piece as indicated on graph.
2: Secure female purse clasp piece according to manufacturer's instructions and as indicated.
3: Folding purse front, back and sides wrong sides together, with teal blue, Whipstitch together; Overcast unfinished edges. Secure male purse clasp piece as indicated.✤

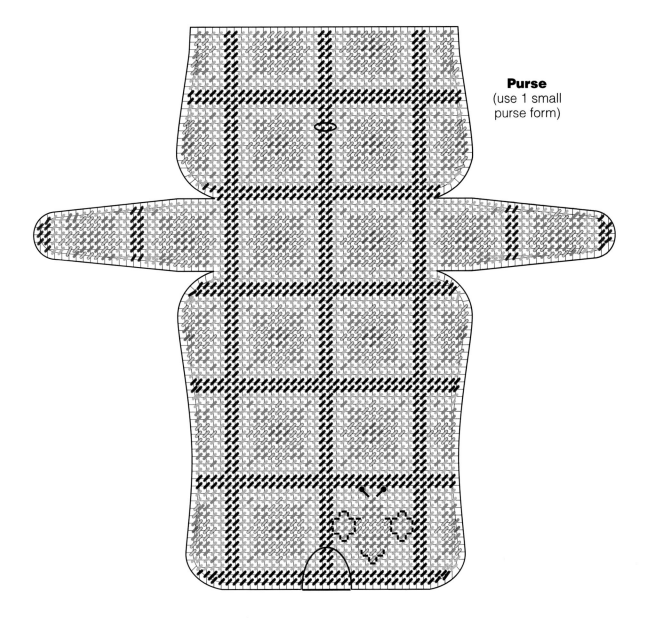

Purse
(use 1 small
purse form)

COLOR KEY: Summertime Clutch

#3 pearl cotton or floss			AMOUNT
■ Black			1 yd. [0.9m]

Worsted-weight	Nylon Plus™	Need-loft®	YARN AMOUNT
Baby Blue	#05	#36	20 yds. [18.3m]
Teal Blue	#08	#50	20 yds. [18.3m]
Fern	#57	#23	18 yds. [16.5m]
Yellow	#26	#57	18 yds. [16.5m]
Bittersweet	#18	#52	8 yds. [7.3m]
Black	#02	#00	1 yd. [0.9m]
White	#01	#41	1 yd. [0.9m]

STITCH KEY:

— Backstitch/Straight
● French Knot
☐ Female Clasp Attachment
☐ Male Clasp Attachment

Hearts & Lace

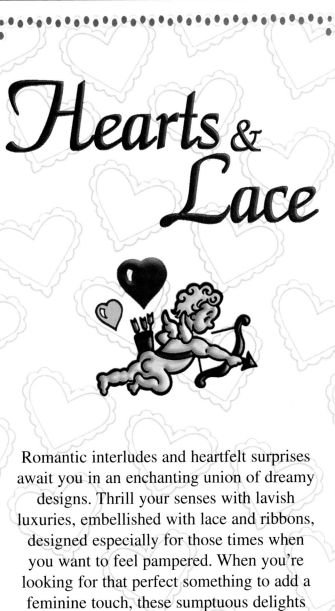

Romantic interludes and heartfelt surprises await you in an enchanting union of dreamy designs. Thrill your senses with lavish luxuries, embellished with lace and ribbons, designed especially for those times when you want to feel pampered. When you're looking for that perfect something to add a feminine touch, these sumptuous delights will tickle your fancy. And don't forget to share the sensation by stitching decorative sentiments for others to show how much you care. Picture frames, sweet little baskets and beribboned bath accessories afford those with a penchant for passion hours of ardent stitching pleasure.

Sweetheart Basket

Designed by Celia Lange Designs

SIZE
5⅛" x 7¾" x 3⅜" tall [13cm x 19.7cm x 8.6cm], not including handle.

SKILL LEVEL: Average

MATERIALS
- ❑ Two sheets of 7-count plastic canvas
- ❑ 1½ yds. [1.4m] of pink ¼" [6mm] satin ribbon
- ❑ Craft glue or glue gun
- ❑ Heavy metallic braid or cord; for amount see Color Key.
- ❑ Worsted-weight or plastic canvas yarn; for amounts see Color Key.

CUTTING INSTRUCTIONS
A: For sides, cut two according to graph.
B: For ends, cut two according to graph.
C: For handle, cut one 5 x 89 holes (no graph).
D: For bottom, cut one 33 x 51 holes (no graph).
E: For hearts, cut two according to graph.

STITCHING INSTRUCTIONS
1: Using colors and stitches indicated, work A, B and E pieces according to graphs; work C and D pieces according to stitch pattern guides. With matching colors, Overcast C and E pieces.
2: With white, Whipstitch A and B pieces together as indicated on graphs; Overcast unfinished top edges. With crimson, Whipstitch D piece to A and B assembly.
NOTE: Cut two 12" [30.5cm] lengths from ribbon. Tie each ribbon into a bow; trim ends as desired.
3: Glue one Heart to center of each bow, glue each bow to handle as shown in photo. Glue handle ends inside Basket as shown.
4: Keeping ribbon flat as you work, weave remaining ribbon around Basket, working over white and under red Long Stitches as indicated on A and B graphs. Trim ribbon ends to fit; Overlap and glue ends to secure.✽

Bottom Stitch Pattern Guide

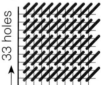

33 holes

51 holes

Continue established pattern up and across entire piece.

COLOR KEY: Sweetheart Basket

Metallic braid or cord			AMOUNT
■ Silver			17 yds. [15.5m]

Worsted-weight	Nylon Plus™	Need-loft®	YARN AMOUNT
▨ White	#01	#41	45 yds. [41.1m]
■ Crimson	#53	#42	35 yds. [32m]

PLACEMENT:
— Ribbon

E – Heart
(cut 2)
7 x 7 holes

B – End (cut 2) 22 x 33 holes

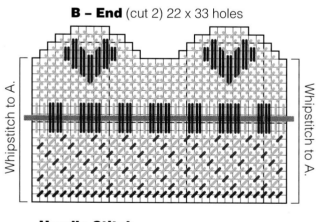

Whipstitch to A.

Whipstitch to A.

Handle Stitch Pattern Guide

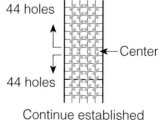

44 holes

← Center

44 holes

Continue established pattern across entire piece.

A – Side (cut 2) 22 x 51 holes

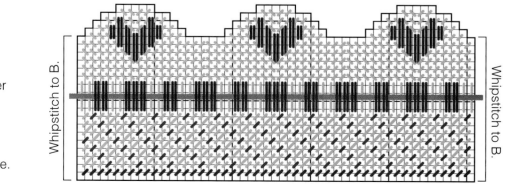

Whipstitch to B.

Whipstitch to B.

Poinsettia Coaster Set

Designed by Joyce Messenger

SIZES

Coasters are 3¼" x 4⅛" [8.3cm x 10.5cm]; Coaster Holder is 4½" x 5¾" x 4" tall [11.4cm x 14.6cm x 10.2cm] including handle. Measurements do not include lace.

SKILL LEVEL: Average

MATERIALS

❑ One sheet of clear and ¼ sheet of white 7-count plastic canvas
❑ 3 yds. [2.7m] of white pre-gathered 1" [2.5cm] lace
❑ Craft glue or glue gun
❑ Heavy metallic braid or cord; for amount see Color Key.
❑ Worsted-weight or plastic canvas yarn; for amounts see Color Key.

CUTTING INSTRUCTIONS

NOTE: B piece is cut from white, remaining pieces are cut from clear canvas.
A: For Coasters and Holder top, cut five (four for Coasters and one for Holder top) according to graph.
B: For Holder bottom, cut one according to graph.
C: For handle, cut one 3 x 70 holes (no graph).

STITCHING INSTRUCTIONS

NOTE: B piece is not worked.
1: Using colors and stitches indicated, work A pieces according to graph; fill in uncoded areas using white and Continental Stitch. With white, Overcast edges.
2: Using red and stitches indicated, work C according to Handle Stitch Pattern Guide; with gold (omit short edges), Overcast edges.
3: For Holder, with white, Whipstitch short ends of C to B as indicated on graph; Overcast unfinished edges.
NOTE: Cut five 14" [35.6cm], one 17" [43.2cm] and one 19" [48.3cm] pieces of lace.
4: Glue one 14" piece of lace around wrong side of each A and 17" piece of lace to right side of B as indicated; glue 19" piece of lace around wrong side of B. Overlap lace ends, glue to secure; trim away excess as needed to fit.
5: Center and glue one A over B.✿

COLOR KEY: Poinsettia Coaster Set

Metallic braid or cord			AMOUNT
■ Gold			3 yds. [2.7m]

Worsted-weight	Nylon Plus™	Need-loft®	YARN AMOUNT
■ Xmas Red	#19	#02	20 yds. [18.3m]
☐ White	#01	#41	18 yds. [16.5m]
▨ Xmas Green	#58	#28	15 yds. [13.7m]

ATTACHMENTS:
☐ Handle
☐ 17" Lace

Handle Stitch Pattern Guide

Continue established pattern across entire piece.

A – Coaster & Holder Top
(cut 5 from clear) 21 x 27 holes

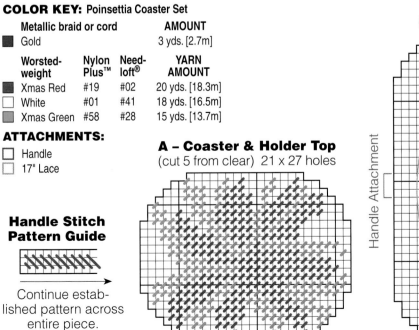

B – Holder Bottom
(cut 1 from white) 30 x 38 holes

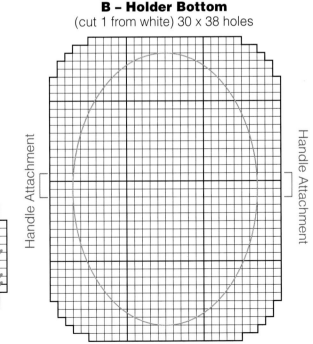

Handle Attachment

Handle Attachment

Bathroom Gift Set

Designed by Betty Frew

SIZES

Dispenser Cover is 2¼" x 3¼" x 5¼" tall [5.7cm x 8.3cm x 13.3cm]; Catch-All is 2¼" x 4⅜" x 3⅛" tall [5.7cm x 11.1cm x 7.9cm]; Basket is 4⅝" x 13½ x 7¾" tall [11.7cm x 34.3cm x 19.7cm], including handle.

SKILL LEVEL: Average

MATERIALS

- Four sheets of 7-count plastic canvas
- 4" [10.2cm] Uniek® plastic canvas circle
- 12" [30.5cm] of dusty rose ⅝" [16mm] satin ribbon
- Worsted-weight or plastic canvas yarn; for amounts see Color Key.

CUTTING INSTRUCTIONS

NOTE: Graphs continued on page 92.
A: For Dispenser Cover side, cut one 34 x 54 holes.
B: For Dispenser Cover bottom, cut one according to graph.
C: For Catch-All back, cut one according to graph.
D: For Catch-All front, cut one according to graph.
E: For Catch-All bottom, cut one from circle according to graph.
F: For Basket sides, cut two according to graph.
G: For Basket ends, cut two 14 x 30 holes.
H: For Basket bottom, cut one 30 x 90 holes (no graph).

STITCHING INSTRUCTIONS

NOTE: B, E and H pieces are not worked.
1: Using colors indicated and Continental Stitch, work A, C, D, F and G pieces according to graphs; fill in uncoded areas with white and Continental Stitch.
2: For Dispenser Cover, with white, Whipstitch ends of A together as indicated on graph; Whipstitch A and B pieces together. Overcast unfinished edges.
3: For Catch-All, with white, Whipstitch C-E pieces together as indicated and according to Catch-All Assembly Illustration; Overcast unfinished edges.
4: For Basket, with white, Whipstitch F-H pieces together as indicated; Overcast unfinished edges.
5: Tie ribbon into a bow around Basket handle as shown in photo.❉

COLOR KEY: Bathroom Gift Set

Worsted-weight	Nylon Plus™	Need-loft®	YARN AMOUNT
☐ White	#01	#41	2½ oz. [70.9g]
▨ Pink	#11	#07	32 yds. [29.3m]
■ Lavender	#12	#05	18 yds. [16.5m]
▨ Mermaid Green	#37	#53	12 yds. [11m]
▨ Lemon	#25	#20	4 yds. [3.7m]

Catch-All Assembly Illustration

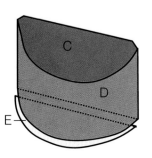

A – Dispenser Cover Side (cut 1) 34 x 54 holes

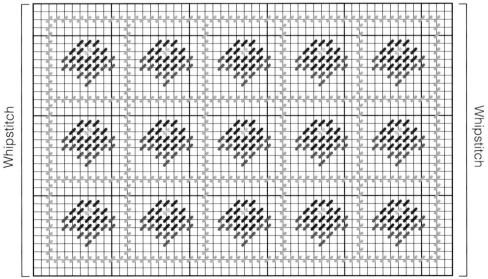

Bathroom Gift Set

Instructions and photo on pages 90 & 91

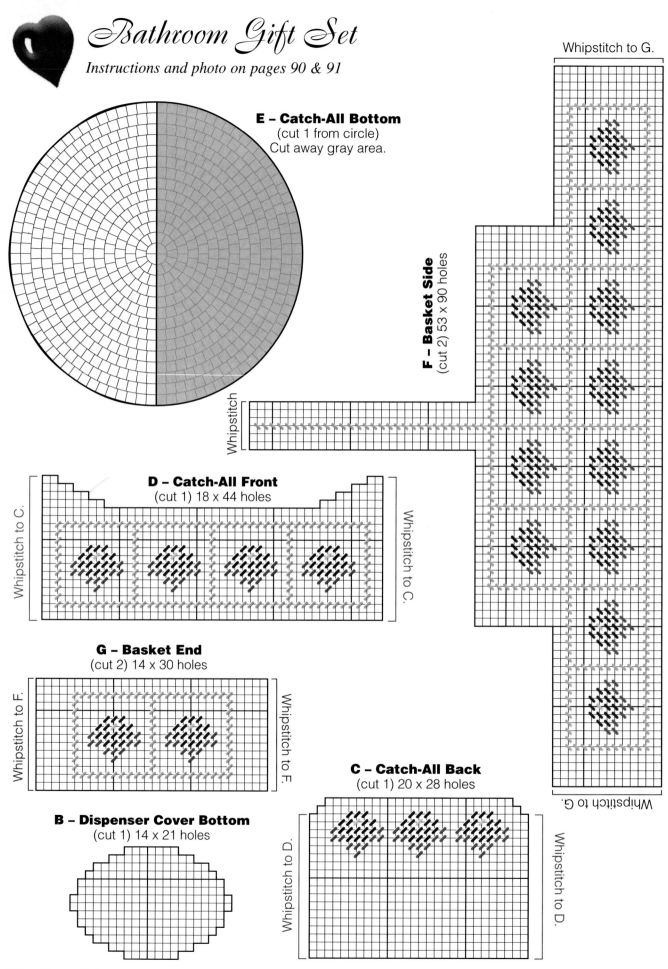

Whipstitch to G.

E – Catch-All Bottom
(cut 1 from circle)
Cut away gray area.

F – Basket Side
(cut 2) 53 x 90 holes

Whipstitch

D – Catch-All Front
(cut 1) 18 x 44 holes

Whipstitch to C.

Whipstitch to C.

G – Basket End
(cut 2) 14 x 30 holes

Whipstitch to F.

Whipstitch to F.

C – Catch-All Back
(cut 1) 20 x 28 holes

Whipstitch to D.

Whipstitch to D.

Whipstitch to G.

B – Dispenser Cover Bottom
(cut 1) 14 x 21 holes

INSTRUCTIONS ON NEXT PAGE

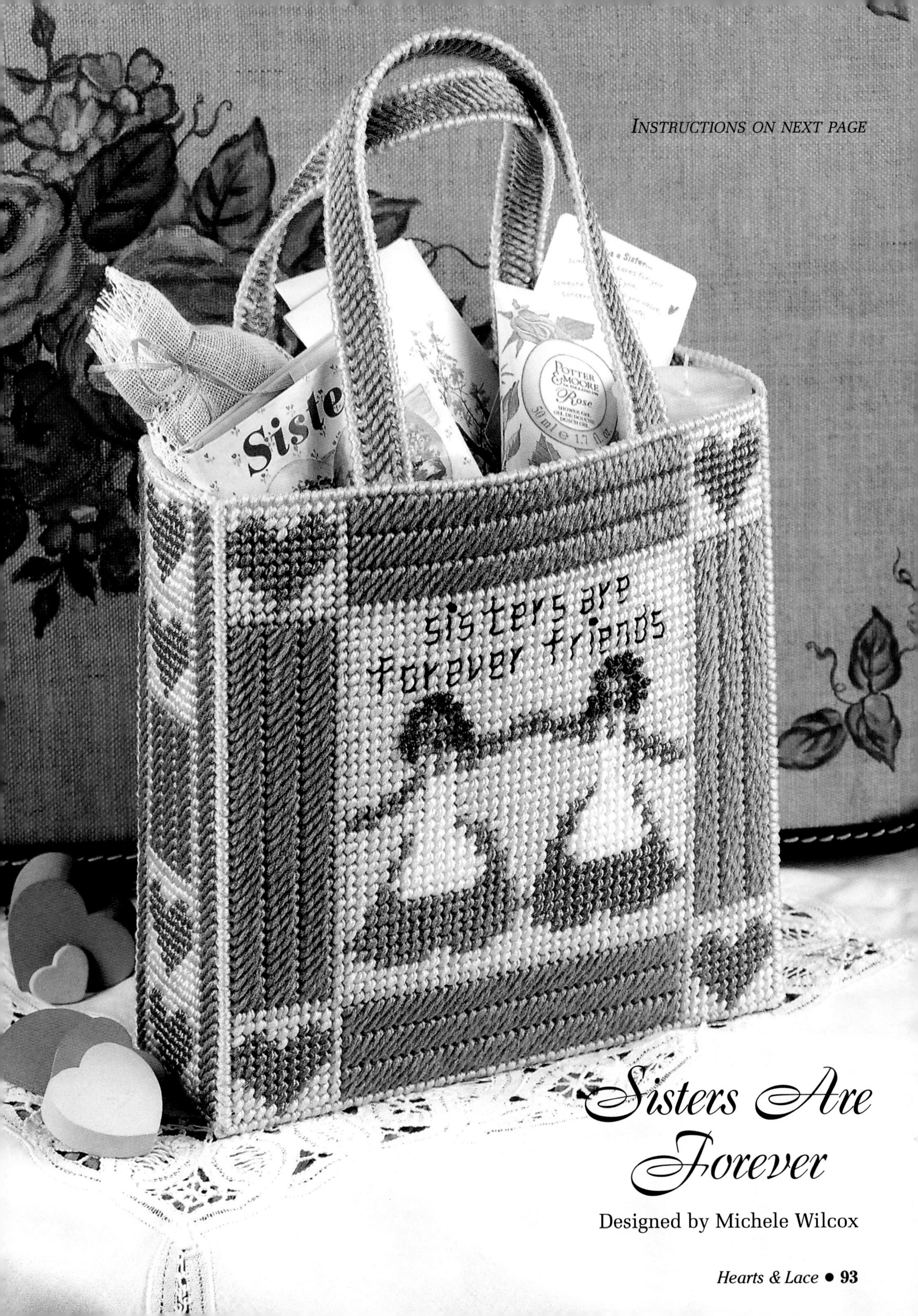

Sisters Are Forever

Designed by Michele Wilcox

Sisters Are Forever

Photo on page 93

SIZE
2⅞" x 8⅜" x 8⅜" [7.3cm x 21.3cm x 21.3cm], not including handles.

SKILL LEVEL: Average

MATERIALS
- ❑ Three sheets of 7-count plastic canvas
- ❑ #5 pearl cotton or six-strand embroidery floss; for amounts see Color Key.
- ❑ Worsted-weight or plastic canvas yarn; for amounts see Color Key.

CUTTING INSTRUCTIONS
A: For sides, cut two 55 x 55 holes.
B: For ends, cut two 18 x 55 holes.
C: For bottom, cut one 18 x 55 holes.
D: For handles, cut two 4 x 90 holes. (no graph).

STITCHING INSTRUCTIONS
1: Using colors and stitches indicated, work A-D pieces according to graphs and Handle Stitch Pattern Guide; fill in uncoded areas using straw and Continental Stitch. With baby green, Overcast D pieces.
2: Using pearl cotton or six strands floss in colors and embroidery stitches indicated, embroider detail on A pieces as indicated on graph.
3: With baby green, Whipstitch A-C pieces together to form tote; Overcast unfinished edges. Glue D pieces inside tote as shown in photo.✷

A – Side
(cut 2) 55 x 55 holes

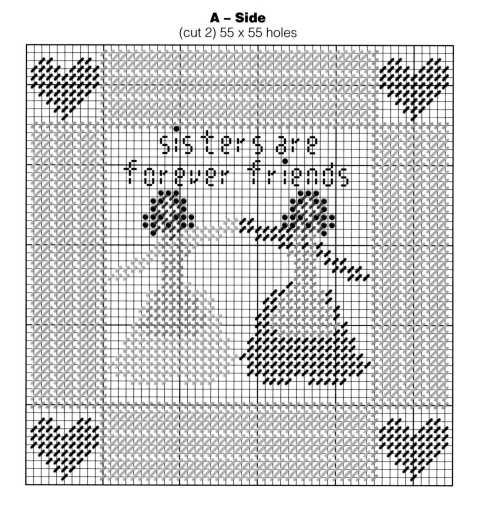

B – End
(cut 2)
18 x 55 holes

C – Bottom
(cut 1)
18 x 55 holes

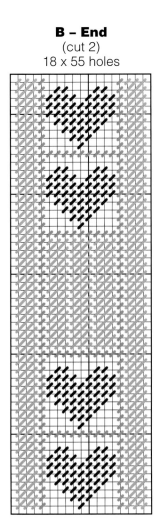

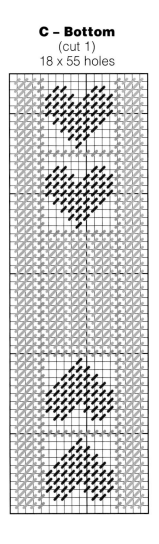

**Handle Stitch
Pattern Guide**

Continue established pattern
across each entire piece.

COLOR KEY: Sisters Are Forever

#5 pearl cotton or floss			AMOUNT
■ Black			6 yds. [5.5m]
■ Brown			4 yds. [3.7m]
■ Blue			1/2 yd. [0.5m]
■ Red			1/2 yd. [0.5m]

Worsted-weight	Nylon Plus™	Need-loft®	YARN AMOUNT
▨ Cerulean	#38	#34	76 yds. [69.5m]
☐ Straw	#41	#19	40 yds. [36.6m]
▨ Baby Green	#28	#26	35 yds. [32m]
■ Lavender	#12	#05	25 yds. [22.9m]
▨ White	#01	#41	6 yds. [5.5m]
▨ Coral	#14	#66	2 yds. [1.8m]

STITCH KEY:

— Backstitch/Straight
● French Knot

Hearts & Lace • **95**

Mother's Helpers

Designed by Pamela Reed Prather

SIZES

Journal Cover fits a ½" x 5¼" x 7⅞" book [1.3cm x 13.3cm x 20cm]; Frame is 6⅜" x 8½" [16.2cm x 21.6cm], not including lace, with a 4" x 6⅛" [10.2cm x 15.6cm] photo window; Candle Ring fits around a 2¾" across [7cm] candle.

SKILL LEVEL: Average

MATERIALS:

❑ Five sheets of 7-count plastic canvas
❑ 2½ yds. [2.3m] of white ¾" [1.9cm] eyelet lace
❑ 12" [30.5cm] of white ⅝" [16mm] satin ribbon
❑ Craft glue or glue gun
❑ Worsted weight or plastic canvas yarn; for amounts see Color Key.

CUTTING INSTRUCTIONS

NOTE: Graphs continued on pages 98 and 99.
A: For Journal Cover front, cut one 37 x 53 holes.
B: For Journal Cover back, cut one 37 x 53 holes.
C: For Journal Cover spine, cut one 6 x 53 holes (no graph).
D: For Journal Cover flaps, cut two 15 x 53 holes (no graph).
E: For Frame front #1, cut one according to graph.
F: For Frame front #2, cut one according to graph.
G: For Frame back, cut one 42 x 56 holes (no graph).
H: For Hearts #1, cut three according to graph.
I: For Hearts #2, cut three according to graph.
J: For Candle Ring, cut one 5 x 61 holes.

STITCHING INSTRUCTIONS

NOTE: D and G pieces are not worked.
1: Using colors and stitches indicated, work A-C, E, F (leave uncoded area unworked) and H-J pieces according to graphs and Spine Stitch Pattern

Guide; with lemon for H and bright purple for I, Overcast edges of H and I pieces.
2: For Journal Cover, with lemon, Whipstitch and assemble A-D and two H pieces according to Cover Assembly Diagram; Overcast unfinished edges.
3: For Frame, with lemon, Whipstitch and assemble E-G and remaining H pieces together according to Frame Assembly Diagram; Overcast unfinished edges. Glue lace to outside edges of G, trim away excess as needed to fit. Hang or display as desired.
4: For Candle Ring, with lemon, Whipstitch short ends of J together as indicated, Overcast unfinished edges.
5: Glue lace around wrong side of each I piece, trim away excess as needed to fit. Glue I pieces to J as shown in photo.✳

A – Journal Cover Front
(cut 1) 37 x 53 holes

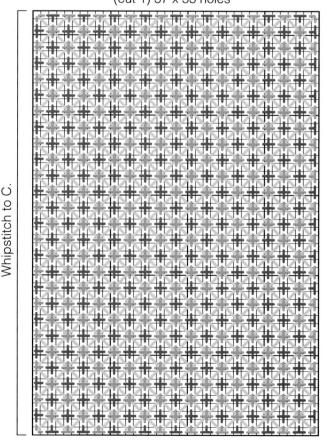

Whipstitch to C.

COLOR KEY: Mother's Helpers

Worsted-weight	Nylon Plus™	Need-loft®	YARN AMOUNT
☐ Straw	#41	#19	3 oz. [85.1g]
■ Bright Purple	–	#64	35 yds. [32m]
▨ Bright Blue	–	#60	30 yds. [27.4m]

ATTACHMENT:
☐ Frame Front #1/#2

B – Journal Cover Back
(cut 1) 37 x 53 holes

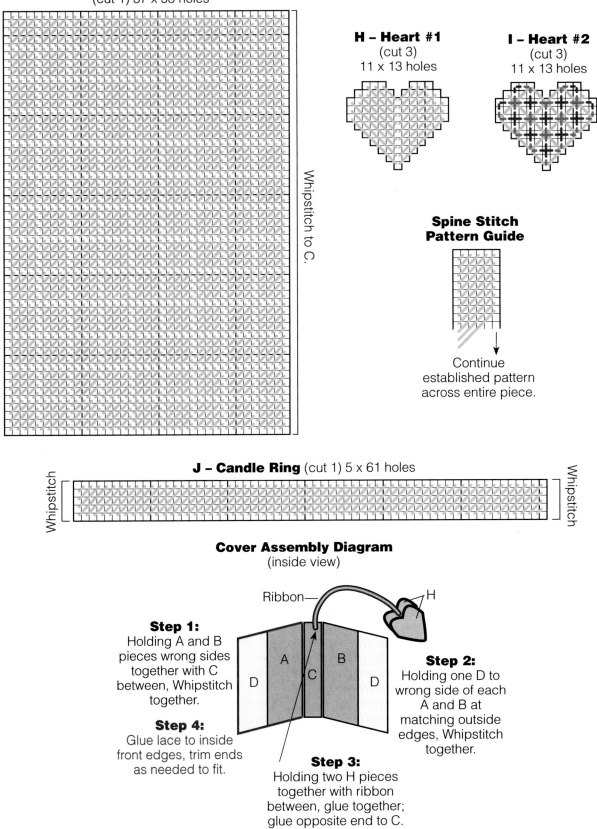

Whipstitch to C.

H – Heart #1
(cut 3)
11 x 13 holes

I – Heart #2
(cut 3)
11 x 13 holes

Spine Stitch Pattern Guide

Continue
established pattern
across entire piece.

J – Candle Ring (cut 1) 5 x 61 holes

Whipstitch

Whipstitch

Cover Assembly Diagram
(inside view)

Ribbon—

H

Step 1:
Holding A and B
pieces wrong sides
together with C
between, Whipstitch
together.

D

A

C

B

D

Step 2:
Holding one D to
wrong side of each
A and B at
matching outside
edges, Whipstitch
together.

Step 4:
Glue lace to inside
front edges, trim ends
as needed to fit.

Step 3:
Holding two H pieces
together with ribbon
between, glue together;
glue opposite end to C.

E – Frame Front #1
(cut 1) 38 x 52 holes

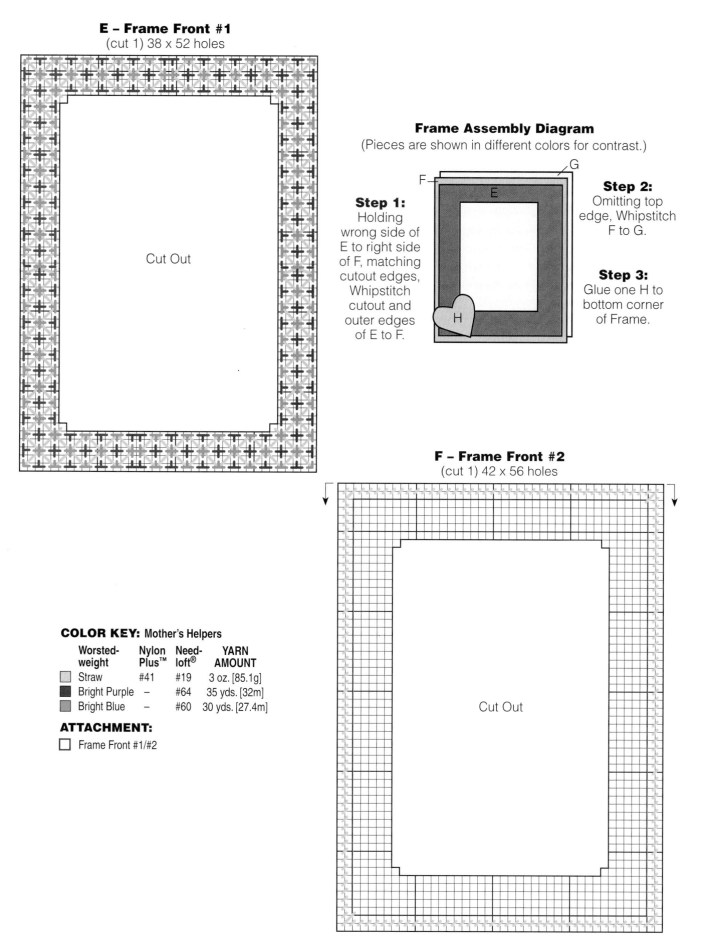

Cut Out

Frame Assembly Diagram
(Pieces are shown in different colors for contrast.)

Step 1:
Holding wrong side of E to right side of F, matching cutout edges, Whipstitch cutout and outer edges of E to F.

E

F

G

H

Step 2:
Omitting top edge, Whipstitch F to G.

Step 3:
Glue one H to bottom corner of Frame.

F – Frame Front #2
(cut 1) 42 x 56 holes

Cut Out

Whipstitch to G between arrows.

COLOR KEY: Mother's Helpers

Worsted-weight	Nylon Plus™	Need-loft®	YARN AMOUNT
☐ Straw	#41	#19	3 oz. [85.1g]
■ Bright Purple	–	#64	35 yds. [32m]
■ Bright Blue	–	#60	30 yds. [27.4m]

ATTACHMENT:

☐ Frame Front #1/#2

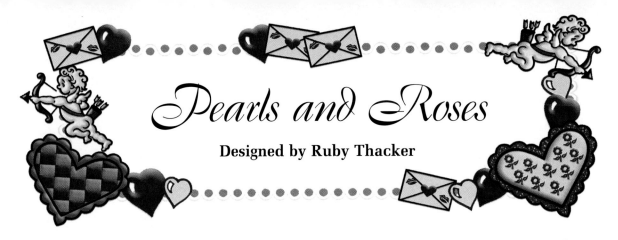

Pearls and Roses

Designed by Ruby Thacker

SIZES

Frame is 6½" x 7½" [16.5cm x 19cm] with a 4¼" x 5" [10.8cm x 12.7cm] photo window; Music Box is 4½" across x 3¾" tall [11.4cm x 9.5cm]. Measurements do not include embellishments.

SKILL LEVEL: Challenging

MATERIALS

❏ Two standard size sheets and scrap of 12" x 18" [11cm x 16.5cm] 7-count plastic canvas
❏ Three Uniek® 4" [10.2cm] plastic canvas circles
❏ 35 white 4mm pearls
❏ Four pearlized rose motifs
❏ Four baby blue 16mm x 12mm Moroccan beads
❏ About 2⅜" x 2" x 1³⁄₁₆" tall [6cm x 5.1cm x 3cm] music box with a bottom wind key
❏ Craft glue or glue gun
❏ Worsted weight or plastic canvas yarn; for amounts see Color Key on page 103.

CUTTING INSTRUCTIONS

NOTES: Graphs continued on pages 102 and 103. Use larger scrap for D piece.

A: For Frame front and back, cut two (one for front and one for back) according to graph.
B: For Frame stand, cut one according to graph.
C: For Music Box lid top, cut one according to graph.
D: For Music Box lid side, cut one 19 x 90 holes.
E: For Music Box side, cut one according to graph.

F: For Music Box bottom, cut two from circles according to graph.
G: For Music Box center floor, cut one from remaining circle according to graph.

STITCHING INSTRUCTIONS

NOTE: Back A, B and F pieces are not worked.
1: Using baby blue and stitches indicated, work front A, C, D and E (overlap ends as indicated on D and E graphs and work through both thicknesses at overlap areas to join) and G pieces according to graphs; Overcast cutout edges of front A.
2: For Frame, Whipstitch A and B pieces together according to Frame Assembly Diagram; Overcast unfinished edges. Glue two motifs to front as shown in photo.
3: For Music Box lid, Whipstitch C and D pieces together; Overcast unfinished edges. Glue remaining motifs to lid as shown.
4: For Music Box, Whipstitch and assemble E-G pieces together according to Music Box Assembly Diagram; Overcast unfinished edges.✽

COLOR KEY: Pearls and Roses

Worsted-weight	Nylon Plus™	Need-loft®	YARN AMOUNT
▨ Baby Blue	#05	#36	3 oz. [85g]

ATTACHMENTS:
O Pearl
☐ Music Box Center Floor/Side
○ Feet

F – Music Box Bottom
(cut 2 from two circles) Cut out gray areas.

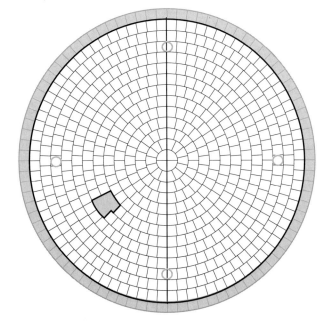

Pearls and Roses

Instructions and photo on page 100 & 101

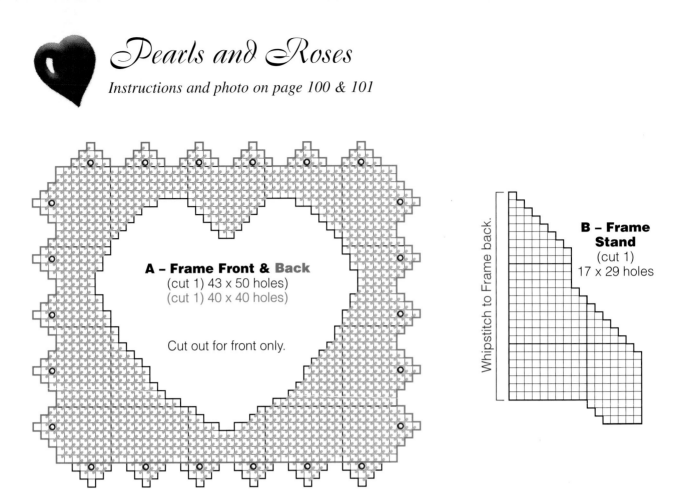

A – Frame Front & Back
(cut 1) 43 x 50 holes)
(cut 1) 40 x 40 holes)

Cut out for front only.

B – Frame Stand
(cut 1)
17 x 29 holes

Whipstitch to Frame back.

ATTACHMENTS:
O Pearl
☐ Music Box Center Floor/Side
○ Feet

G – Music Box Center Floor
(cut away 1 outer row from one circle)

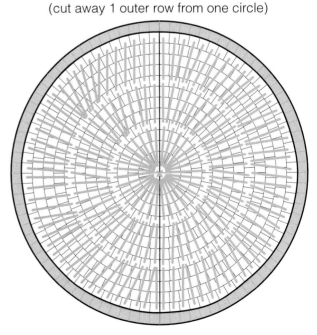

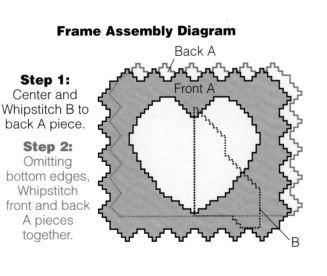

Frame Assembly Diagram

Back A

Front A

Step 1:
Center and Whipstitch B to back A piece.

Step 2:
Omitting bottom edges, Whipstitch front and back A pieces together.

B

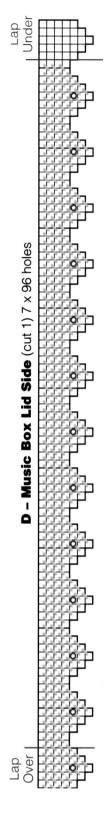

D – Music Box Lid Side (cut 1) 7 x 96 holes

C – Music Box Lid Top
(cut 1) 29 x 29 holes

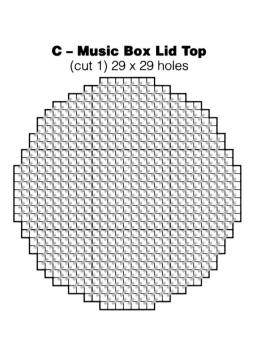

COLOR KEY: Pearls and Roses

	Worsted-weight	Nylon Plus™	Need-loft®	YARN AMOUNT
	Baby Blue	#05	#36	3 oz. [85g]

ATTACHMENTS:
- O Pearl
- ☐ Music Box Center Floor/Side
- ◌ Feet

E – Music Box Side (cut 1) 19 x 90 holes

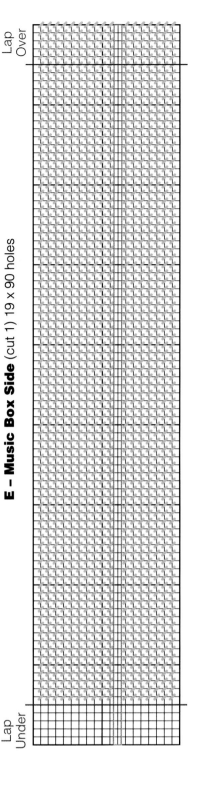

Music Box Assembly Diagram
(Pieces are shown in different colors for contrast, gray denotes wrong side.)

Step 1:
Whipstitch E and G pieces together.

Step 2:
Holding two F pieces together matching cutout edges, anchor music box in center; insert key through cutouts and screw into music box.

Step 3:
Whipstitch F and E pieces together; work through all thicknesses as one.

Step 4:
For feet, glue beads to bottom of F.

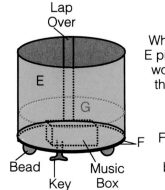

Swan Tissue Cover

Designed by Michele Wilcox

SIZE

Snugly covers a boutique-style tissue box.

SKILL LEVEL: Average

MATERIALS

- ❏ 1¼ sheets of 7-count plastic canvas
- ❏ #5 pearl cotton or six-strand embroidery floss; for amount see Color Key.
- ❏ Worsted weight or plastic canvas yarn; for amounts see Color Key.

CUTTING INSTRUCTIONS

A: For sides, cut four 30 x 36 holes.

B: For top, cut one according to graph.

STITCHING INSTRUCTIONS

1: Using colors and stitches indicated, work pieces according to graphs; with turquoise, Overcast cutout edges of B piece.

2: Using pearl cotton or six strands floss and embroidery stitches indicated, embroider detail on A pieces as indicated on graph.

3: With turquoise, Whipstitch A and B pieces together to form Cover; Overcast unfinished edges.❋

COLOR KEY: Swan Tissue Cover

#5 pearl cotton or floss			AMOUNT
■ Black			15 yds. [13.7m]

Worsted-weight	Nylon Plus™	Need-loft®	YARN AMOUNT
■ Fern	#57	#23	30 yds. [27.4m]
■ White	#01	#41	30 yds. [27.4m]
■ Turquoise	#03	#54	22 yds. [20.1m]
■ Aqua Light	#39	#49	18 yds. [16.5m]
■ Straw	#41	#19	15 yds. [13.7m]
■ Black	#02	#00	1 yd. [0.9m]
■ Tangerine	#15	#11	1 yd. [0.9m]

STITCH KEY:

- — Backstitch/Straight
- • French Knot

A – Side
(cut 4) 30 x 36 holes

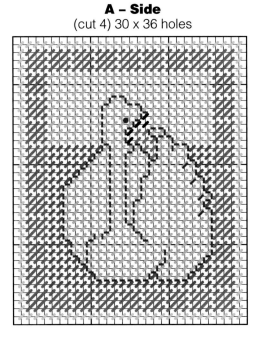

B – Top
(cut 1) 30 x 30 holes

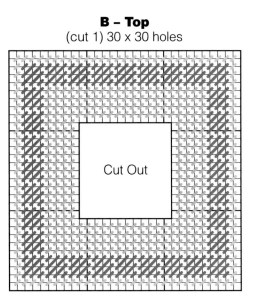

'Tis the Season

Make your list but don't check it twice, because these festive ornaments are nothing but nice! Overflowing with brilliant colors, sparkling jewels and radiant ribbons, this generous presentation is sure to fulfill all your holiday crafting wishes. Wrap your home in heartfelt happiness with these enduring designs guaranteed to bring renewed joy to your most special holiday celebrations. Don your elf hat and get a jump on your Christmas stitching now, then watch little eyes shine with glee when they behold whimsical figures, tiny angels, gingerbread houses and more illuminating the tree.

Garlands Galore

Designed by Kristine Loffredo

SIZE
Each is about 40" [101.6cm] long.

SKILL LEVEL: Easy

MATERIALS FOR BOTH
- ❑ Two sheets of 7-count plastic canvas
- ❑ 48 gold 6mm beads
- ❑ 16 gold ⅞" [2.2cm] leaf spangles
- ❑ Beading needle and white sewing thread
- ❑ Worsted weight or plastic canvas yarn; for amounts see individual Color Keys.

CUTTING INSTRUCTIONS
A: For hearts, cut five according to graph.
B: For trees, cut four according to graph.
C: For houses, cut four according to graph.
D: For stars, cut thirteen according to graph.
E: For angels, cut eight according to graph.

SPARKLE GARLAND STITCHING INSTRUCTIONS
1: Using colors indicated and Continental Stitch, work A-C and four D pieces according to graphs; with matching colors, Overcast edges of pieces.
2: With thread and alternating A-D pieces, sew three beads between each piece at ▲ holes as indicated and according to Sparkle Garland Assembly Illustration.

ANGEL GARLAND STITCHING INSTRUCTIONS
1: Using colors and stitches indicated, work nine D and E pieces according to graphs; with matching colors, Overcast edges of pieces.
2: For wings, with thread, sew one spangle to each ✦ hole on wrong side of each E as indicated on graph.
3: With tan yarn and alternating pieces, tack D and E pieces together at ▲ holes as indicated.❊

COLOR KEY: Angel Garland

	Worsted-weight	Nylon Plus™	Need-loft®	YARN AMOUNT
	Yellow	#26	#57	18 yds. [16.5m]
	White	#01	#41	16 yds. [14.6m]
	Tan	#33	#18	8 yds. [7.3m]
▨	Baby Yellow	#42	#21	6 yds. [5.5m]

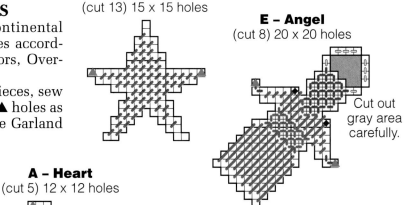

D – Star
(cut 13) 15 x 15 holes

E – Angel
(cut 8) 20 x 20 holes

Cut out gray area carefully.

A – Heart
(cut 5) 12 x 12 holes

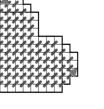

B – Tree
(cut 4) 15 x 15 holes

C – House
(cut 4) 14 x 17 holes

COLOR KEY: Sparkle Garland

	Worsted-weight	Nylon Plus™	Need-loft®	YARN AMOUNT
■	Xmas Red	#19	#02	18 yds. [16.5m]
▨	Holly	#31	#27	16 yds. [14.6m]

Sparkle Garland Assembly Illustration

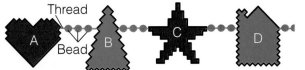

Thread

A   B   C   D

Bead

Sparkling Snowflakes

Designed by Mary T. Cosgrove

SIZES

Photo Snowflake is 5" x 5½" [12.7cm x 14cm] with a 2⅝" x 3" [6.7cm x 7.6cm] photo window; Glow Snowflake is 5" x 5½" [12.7cm x 14cm].

SKILL LEVEL: Easy

MATERIALS

❑ Two Uniek® 5" [12.7cm] plastic canvas hexagon shapes
❑ 14-count metallic perforated paper
❑ Small photo of choice
❑ Craft glue or glue gun
❑ ⅛" [3mm] metallic ribbon; for amounts see Color Key.
❑ Metallic cord; for amounts see Color Key.

CUTTING INSTRUCTIONS

A: For Photo Snowflake, cut one from one hexagon shape according to graph.
B: For Glow Snowflake, cut one from one hexagon shape according to graph on page 112.
C: For Photo Snowflake backing, cut one from metallic perforated paper according to graph.

STITCHING INSTRUCTIONS

NOTE: Use a doubled strand of ⅛" ribbon.
1: Using colors indicated and Cross Stitch, work A and B pieces according to graphs. With gold, Overcast edges of A; with grapefruit for center cutout as indicated on graph and with blue, Overcast edges of B.
2: For Photo Snowflake, trim photo to fit photo window and glue to wrong side of A; Glue C to wrong side of A over photo.
3: Hang or display as desired.✳

A – Photo Snowflake
(cut 1 from 1 hexagon shape)

Cut away gray areas carefully.

C – Backing
(cut 1 from perforated paper)

COLOR KEY: Sparkling Snowflakes

⅛" ribbon	Kreinik	AMOUNT
☐ Blue	006	18 yds. [16.5m]
▨ Grapefruit	052F	16 yds. [14.6m]
▨ Pearl	032	14 yds. [12.8m]
Metallic cord		**AMOUNT**
☐ Gold		8 yds. [7.3m]

Sparkling Snowflakes

Instructions and photo on pages 110 & 111

B – Glow Snowflake
(cut 1 from 1 hexagon shape)

Overcast with
grapefruit.

Cut away gray areas carefully.

COLOR KEY: Sparkling Snowflakes

1/8" ribbon	Kreinik	AMOUNT
☐ Blue	006	18 yds. [16.5m]
⊘ Grapefruit	052F	16 yds. [14.6m]
⊘ Pearl	032	14 yds. [12.8m]
Metallic cord		**AMOUNT**
☐ Gold		8 yds. [7.3m]

INSTRUCTIONS ON NEXT PAGE

Winter Warmers

Designed by Nancy Marshall

Winter Warmers

Photo on page 113

SIZES

Each Mitten is 3¾" x 5⅛" [9.5cm x 13cm];
Large Teapot is 4⅜" x 4½" [11.1cm x 11.4cm];
Small Teapot is 3¼" x 4" [8.3cm x 10.2cm].

SKILL LEVEL: Average

MATERIALS

❑ Two sheets of 7-count plastic canvas
❑ Worsted weight or plastic canvas yarn; for amounts see Color Key.

CUTTING INSTRUCTIONS

A: For striped mitten sides #1 and #2, cut one each according to graphs.

B: For checkered mitten sides #1 and #2, cut one each according to graphs.

C: For diamond mitten sides #1 and #2, cut one each according to graphs.

D: For small teapot sides #1 and #2, cut one each according to graphs.

E: For large teapot sides #1 and #2, cut one each according to graphs.

STITCHING INSTRUCTIONS

1: Using colors and stitches indicated, work pieces according to graphs.

2: Using gray and Straight Stitch, embroider detail on D pieces as indicated on graphs.

3: For each mitten, holding corresponding pieces wrong sides together, with matching colors, Whipstitch indicated edges together; Overcast unfinished top edges. For each teapot, with indicated and matching colors, Whipstitch corresponding pieces wrong sides together.

4: Hang or display as desired.✳

E – Large Teapot Side #1
(cut 1) 28 x 28 holes

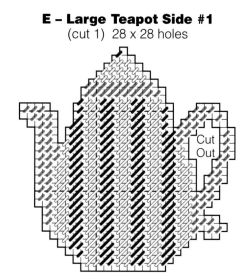

E – Large Teapot Side #2
(cut 1) 28 x 28 holes

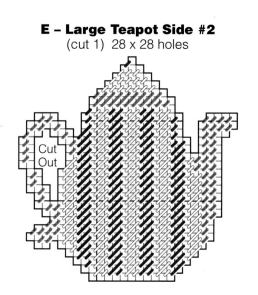

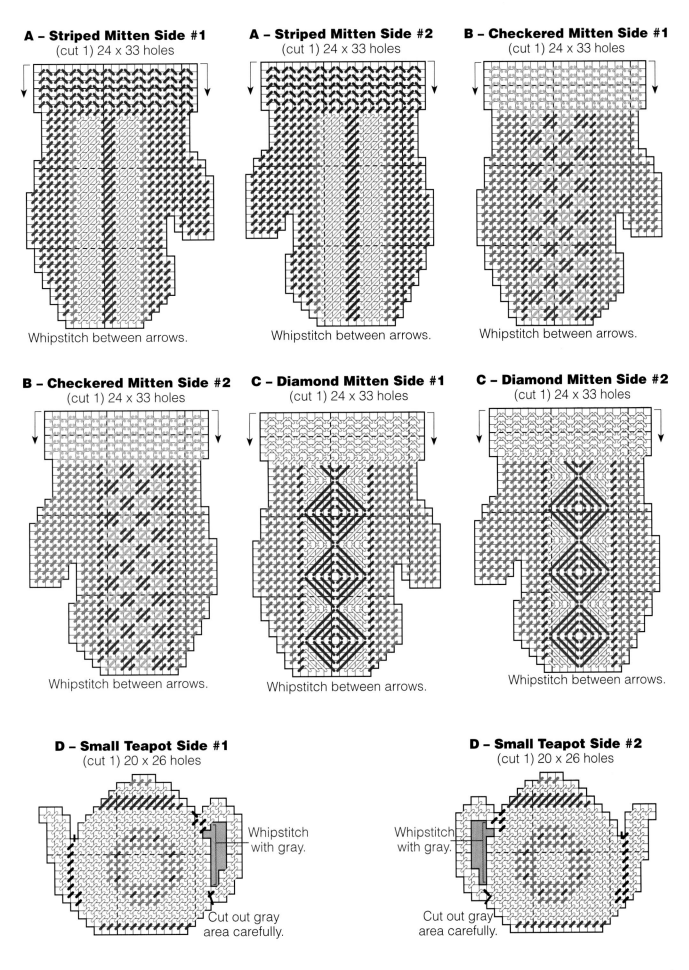

A – Striped Mitten Side #1
(cut 1) 24 x 33 holes

Whipstitch between arrows.

A – Striped Mitten Side #2
(cut 1) 24 x 33 holes

Whipstitch between arrows.

B – Checkered Mitten Side #1
(cut 1) 24 x 33 holes

Whipstitch between arrows.

B – Checkered Mitten Side #2
(cut 1) 24 x 33 holes

Whipstitch between arrows.

C – Diamond Mitten Side #1
(cut 1) 24 x 33 holes

Whipstitch between arrows.

C – Diamond Mitten Side #2
(cut 1) 24 x 33 holes

Whipstitch between arrows.

D – Small Teapot Side #1
(cut 1) 20 x 26 holes

Whipstitch
with gray.

Cut out gray
area carefully.

D – Small Teapot Side #2
(cut 1) 20 x 26 holes

Whipstitch
with gray.

Cut out gray
area carefully.

Toy Shop Santas

Designed by Sandra Miller Maxfield

SIZES

Train Santa is 5½" x 7" [14cm x 17.8cm]; Skateboard Santa is 3⅛" x 5¾" [7.9cm x 14.6cm]; Rocking Horse Santa is 4¾" x 5¾" [12.1cm x 14.6cm].

SKILL LEVEL: Average

MATERIALS

❑ One sheet of 7-count plastic canvas
❑ Craft glue or glue gun
❑ Worsted weight or plastic canvas yarn; for amounts see Color Key on page 118.

CUTTING INSTRUCTIONS

NOTE: Graphs on page 118.

A: For bodies, cut three according to graph.
B: For heads, cut three according to graph.
C: For hats, cut three according to graph.
D: For legs #1 and #2, cut number indicated according to graphs.
E: For arms #1 and #2, cut three each according to graphs.
F: For train, cut one according to graph.

G: For train wheels, cut two according to graph.
H: For cowcatcher, cut one according to graph.
I: For rocking horse, cut one according to graph.
J: For skateboard, cut one 2 x 19 holes.
K: For skateboard wheels, cut four according to graph.

STITCHING INSTRUCTIONS

1: Using colors and stitches indicated, work pieces according to graphs; with Xmas red for train and with matching colors, Overcast edges of pieces.
2: Using colors (Separate into individual plies, if desired.) indicated and Straight Stitch, embroider detail on B pieces as indicated on graph.
NOTE: Cut one 2½" [6.4cm] and one 1½" [3.8cm] length of holly.
3: For halter, wrap cut strands over horse's head as indicated on I graph and glue ends at back to secure.
4: Glue pieces together as indicated and according to individual assembly illustrations and as shown in photo.✣

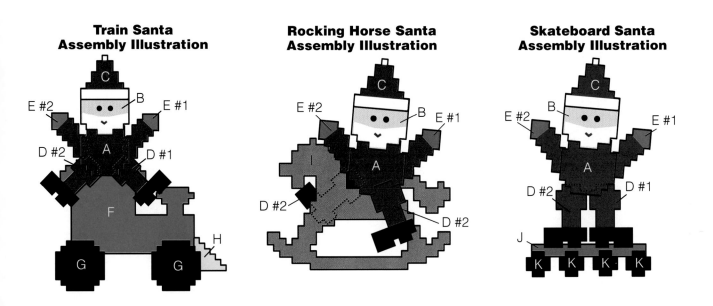

Train Santa Assembly Illustration

Rocking Horse Santa Assembly Illustration

Skateboard Santa Assembly Illustration

A – Body
(cut 3)
9 x 10 holes

B – Head
(cut 3)
8 x 9 holes

C – Hat
(cut 3)
8 x 9 holes

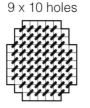

D – Leg #1
(cut 2)
7 x 10 holes

D – Leg #2
(cut 4)
7 x 10 holes

E – Arm #1
(cut 3)
7 x 8 holes

E – Arm #2
(cut 3)
7 x 8 holes

F – Train
(cut 1) 17 x 25 holes

Glue
to H.

G – Train Wheel
(cut 2) 9 x 9 holes

H – Cowcatcher
(cut 1) 6 x 6 holes

Glue to F.

J – Skateboard
(cut 1) 2 x 19 holes

K – Skateboard Wheel
(cut 4)
4 x 4 holes

I – Rocking Horse
(cut 1) 21 x 30 holes

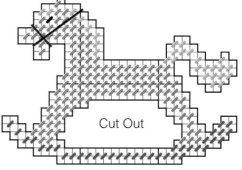

Cut Out

COLOR KEY: Toy Shop Santas

	Worsted-weight	Nylon Plus™	Need-loft®	YARN AMOUNT
■	Xmas Red	#19	#02	24 yds. [21.9m]
■	Black	#02	#00	9 yds. [8.2m]
■	Holly	#31	#27	9 yds. [8.2m]
■	White	#01	#41	8 yds. [7.3m]
■	Camel	#34	#43	5 yds. [4.6m]
■	Beige	#43	#40	3 yds. [2.7m]
■	Cinnamon	#44	#14	3 yds. [2.7m]
▨	Yellow	#26	#57	3 yds. [2.7m]
■	Flesh Tone	–	#56	1 yd. [0.9m]
■	Coral	#14	#66	½ yd. [0.5m]

STITCH KEY:

- ▬ Backstitch/Straight
- ☐ 2½" Strand
- ☐ 1½" Strand

INSTRUCTIONS ON NEXT PAGE

Yuletide Birdhouses

Designed by Kimberly A. Suber

Yuletide Birdhouses

Photo on page 119

SIZE

Each is 3⅝" x 4½" [9.2cm x 11.4cm], not including cross on Church house.

SKILL LEVEL: Average

MATERIALS FOR SET

- ❑ One sheet of 7-count plastic canvas
- ❑ Three gold 6mm beads
- ❑ Seven desired-color ⅜" [10mm] buttons
- ❑ Craft glue or glue gun
- ❑ Metallic cord; for amount see Color Key.
- ❑ Worsted weight or plastic canvas yarn; for amounts see Color Key.

CUTTING INSTRUCTIONS

A: For houses, cut one each according to graphs.

B: For roofs, cut three according to graph.

C: For Church House door, cut one 9 x 10 holes.

D: For Church House windows, cut two according to graph.

E: For cross, cut one according to graph.

F: For Gingerbread House door, cut one according to graph.

G: For candy canes #1 and #2, cut one each according to graphs.

H: For snowman, cut one according to graph.

I: For snowman hat, cut one according to graph.

J: For snowman arms, cut two according to graph.

K: For tree, cut one according to graph.

L: For star, cut one according to graph.

STITCHING INSTRUCTIONS

1: Using colors and stitches indicated, work A, one B, C, D, F-I, K and L pieces according to graphs; substituting turquoise and white for royal, work one of each remaining B in each color according to graph.

2: With royal for Church House, white for Gingerbread House and turquoise for Snowman House, Overcast cutout edges of A pieces; with cord for cross, cinnamon for snowman arms and tree trunk, black for church windows, red for candy canes and with matching colors, Overcast outer edges of pieces.

3: Using colors and embroidery stitches indicated, embroider detail on C, H and K pieces as indicated on graphs.

NOTE: Cut two 9" [22.9cm] and two 3" [7.6cm] lengths each of purple and yellow.

4: For snowman hat band, holding 3" purple and yellow strands together, twist together tightly and wrap around hat as shown in photo; trim ends and glue ends to wrong side of hat to secure.

5: For snowman's scarf, loosely twist 9" strands together; tie around neck area as shown. Tie a knot in each end of scarf; trim ends if desired and fray to fluff.

6: Glue beads, buttons and pieces together as indicated and according to individual assembly illustrations and as shown in photo.

7: Hang or display as desired.✽

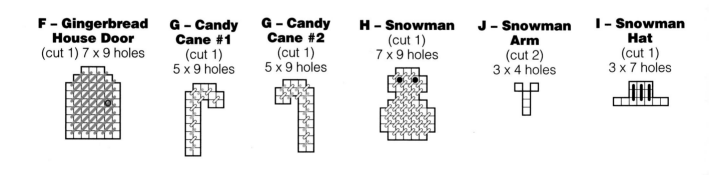

F – Gingerbread House Door
(cut 1) 7 x 9 holes

G – Candy Cane #1
(cut 1)
5 x 9 holes

G – Candy Cane #2
(cut 1)
5 x 9 holes

H – Snowman
(cut 1)
7 x 9 holes

J – Snowman Arm
(cut 2)
3 x 4 holes

I – Snowman Hat
(cut 1)
3 x 7 holes

A – Church House
(cut 1) 19 x 28 holes

Cut out gray area carefully.

A – Gingerbread House
(cut 1) 19 x 28 holes

Cut out gray area carefully.

COLOR KEY: Yuletide Birdhouses

	Metallic cord			AMOUNT
☐	Gold			½ yd. [0.5m]

	Worsted-weight	Nylon Plus™	Need-loft®	YARN AMOUNT
▨	White	#01	#41	17 yds. [15.5m]
■	Cinnamon	#44	#14	10 yds. [9.1m]
▦	Baby Blue	#05	#36	9 yds. [8.2m]
■	Royal	#09	#32	7 yds. [6.4m]
☐	Turquoise	#03	#54	5 yds. [4.6m]
▦	Holly	#31	#27	4 yds. [3.7m]
▨	Red	#20	#01	4 yds. [3.7m]
■	Black	#02	#00	2 yds. [1.8m]
■	Purple	#21	#46	2 yds. [1.8m]
▨	Yellow	#26	#57	2 yds. [1.8m]
▨	Fern	#57	#23	½ yd. [0.5m]

STITCH KEY:
— Backstitch/Straight
● French Knot
○ Bead Placement

A – Snowman House
(cut 1) 19 x 28 holes

Cut out gray area carefully.

C – Church House Door
(cut 1)
9 x 10 holes

E – Cross
(cut 1)
5 x 7 holes

B – Roof
(cut 3) 17 x 17 holes

D – Church House Window
(cut 2)
4 x 5 holes

K – Tree
(cut 1)
7 x 9 holes

L – Star
(cut 1)
3 x 3 holes

Church House Assembly Illustration

Gingerbread House Assembly Illustration

Snowman House Assembly Illustration

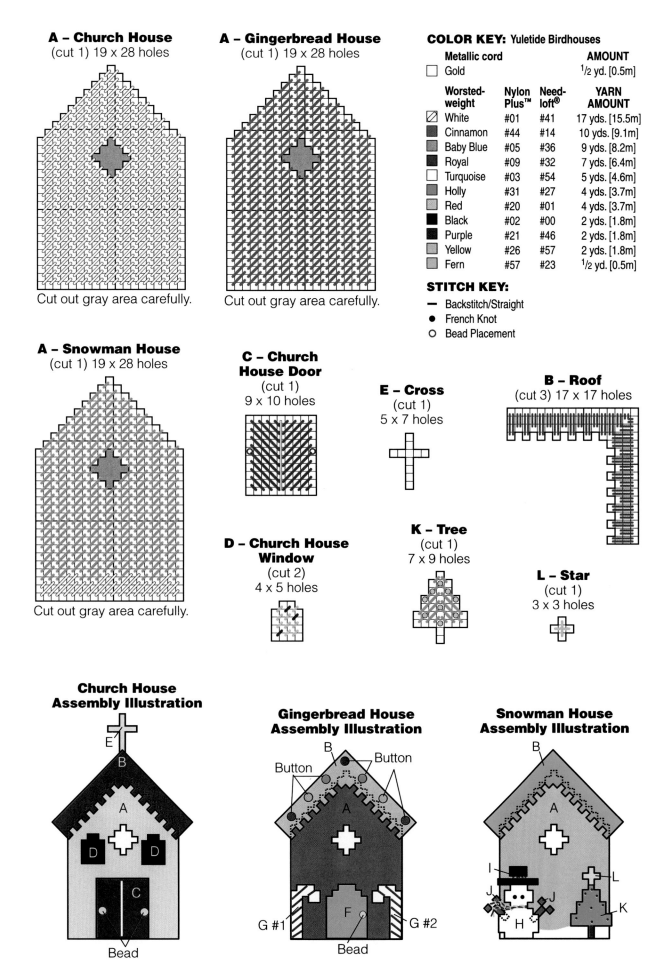

Twilight Pals

Designed by Debbie Tabor

SIZE
About 12" [30.5cm] long, assembled.

SKILL LEVEL: Average

MATERIALS
- ❑ One sheet of 10-count plastic canvas
- ❑ 1 yd. [0.9m] red ¼" [6mm] satin ribbon
- ❑ Two gold ⅝" [16mm] jingle bells
- ❑ Craft glue or glue gun
- ❑ Metallic blending filament; for amount see Color Key.
- ❑ Six-strand rayon embroidery floss; for amounts see Color Key.
- ❑ Six-strand cotton embroidery floss; for amounts see Color Key.

CUTTING INSTRUCTIONS
NOTE: Graphs on page 124.

A: For moon, cut one according to graph.

B: For star, cut one according to graph.

STITCHING INSTRUCTIONS
1: Using six strands floss in colors and stitches indicated, work pieces according to graphs; fill in uncoded area of A using white and Continental Stitch. With matching colors, Overcast edges of pieces.

2: Using one strand blending filament and Straight Stitch, embroider detail over white Continental Stitches on A as indicated on graph. Using cotton floss in colors and embroidery stitches indicated (For French Knots, wrap floss around needle three times.), embroider detail on pieces as indicated.

3: Fold ribbon in half; tie a knot 3" [7.6cm] from fold. Glue pieces, ribbon and bells together according to Twilight Pals Assembly Illustration on page 124.❋

COLOR KEY: Twilight Pals

	Metallic blending filament		JPC®		AMOUNT
	Pearl		1001		7 yds. [6.4m]
	Six strands rayon floss	DMC®	JPC®	Anchor®	AMOUNT
	Bright Red	#666	#3046	#46	4 yds. [3.7m]
	Very Dark Emerald Green	#909	#6228	#923	3 yds. [2.7m]
	One strand cotton floss				AMOUNT
	Black	#310	#8403	#403	4 yds. [3.7m]
	White	White	#1001	#2	¼ yd. [0.2m]
	Two strands cotton floss				AMOUNT
	Black	#310	#8403	#403	4 yds. [3.7m]
	Six strands cotton floss				AMOUNT
	Cream	#712	#1002	#926	3 yds. [2.7m]
	Black	#310	#3403	#403	2 yds. [1.8m]
	White	White	#1001	#2	2 yds. [1.8m]
	Light Baby Pink	#819	#3280	#271	1½ yds. [1.4m]
	Baby Pink	#818	#3281	#23	½ yd. [0.5m]

STITCH KEY:
- — Backstitch/Straight
- • French Knot

Twilight Pals

Instructions and photo on pages 122 & 123

A – Moon
(cut 1) 27 x 30 holes

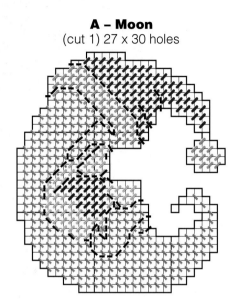

B – Star
(cut 1) 25 x 31 holes

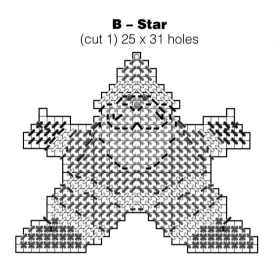

**Twilight Pals
Assembly Illustration**

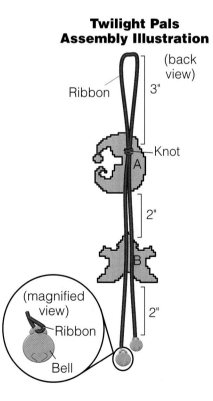

(back view)

Ribbon

3"

Knot

A

2"

B

2"

(magnified view)

Ribbon

Bell

COLOR KEY: Twilight Pals

	Metallic blending filament		JPC®		AMOUNT
�	Pearl		1001		7 yds. [6.4m]
	Six strands rayon floss	DMC®	JPC®	Anchor®	AMOUNT
■	Bright Red	#666	#3046	#46	4 yds. [3.7m]
■	Very Dark Emerald Green	#909	#6228	#923	3 yds. [2.7m]
	One strand cotton floss				AMOUNT
■	Black	#310	#8403	#403	4 yds. [3.7m]
■	White	White	#1001	#2	1/4 yd. [0.2m]
	Two strands cotton floss				AMOUNT
■	Black	#310	#8403	#403	4 yds. [3.7m]
	Six strands cotton floss				AMOUNT
▦	Cream	#712	#1002	#926	3 yds. [2.7m]
▦	Black	#310	#3403	#403	2 yds. [1.8m]
◻	White	White	#1001	#2	2 yds. [1.8m]
▩	Light Baby Pink	#819	#3280	#271	1 1/2 yds. [1.4m]
■	Baby Pink	#818	#3281	#23	1/2 yd. [0.5m]

STITCH KEY:
- — Backstitch/Straight
- • French Knot

INSTRUCTIONS ON NEXT PAGE

Festive Stockings

Designed by Kimberly A. Suber

Festive Stockings

Photo on page 125

SIZE
Each is 2" x 2⅝" [5.1cm x 6.7cm].

SKILL LEVEL: Easy

MATERIALS
- ½ sheet of 7-count plastic canvas
- Scraps of 10-count plastic canvas
- Three sapphire and two crystal 5mm round acrylic faceted stones
- One gold 3mm bead
- Craft glue or glue gun
- Worsted weight or plastic canvas yarn; for amounts see Color Key.

CUTTING INSTRUCTIONS
A: For blue stocking sides #1 and #2, cut one each from 7-count according to graphs.

B: For green stocking sides #1 and #2, cut one each from 7-count according to graphs.

C: For red stocking sides #1 and #2, cut one each from 7-count according to graphs.

D: For poinsettia petals, cut two from 10-count according to graph.

E: For holly, cut one from 10-count according to graph.

STITCHING INSTRUCTIONS
1: Using colors and stitches indicated, work A-C pieces according to graphs. For each stocking, with eggshell for cuffs and with indicated color, Whipstitch corresponding pieces wrong sides together as indicated; with eggshell, Overcast unfinished edges.

NOTE: Separate remaining Xmas red and fern into 2-ply or nylon plastic canvas yarn into 1-ply strands.

2: With 2-ply (or 1-ply) Xmas red for poinsettia petals and holly berry as indicated and with 2-ply (or 1-ply) fern, Overcast edges of D and E pieces.

3: Glue D pieces and bead together according to Poinsettia Assembly Illustration; glue to cuff of green stocking as shown in photo. Glue holly to red stocking and stones to one cuff side on blue stocking as shown.

4: Hang or display as desired.✣

A – Blue Stocking Side #1
(cut 1 from 7-count)
13 x 17 holes

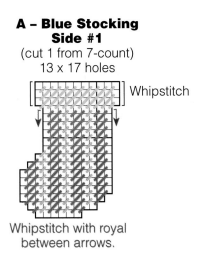

Whipstitch

Whipstitch with royal between arrows.

A – Blue Stocking Side #2
(cut 1 from 7-count)
13 x 17 holes

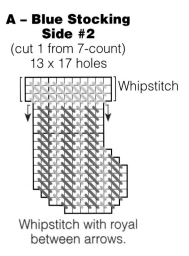

Whipstitch

Whipstitch with royal between arrows.

B – Green Stocking
Side #1
(cut 1 from 7-count)
13 x 17 holes

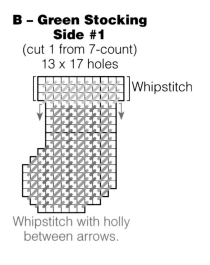

Whipstitch

Whipstitch with holly
between arrows.

B – Green Stocking
Side #2
(cut 1 from 7-count)
13 x 17 holes

Whipstitch

Whipstitch with holly
between arrows.

C – Red Stocking
Side #1
(cut 1 from 7-count)
13 x 17 holes

Whipstitch

Whipstitch with red
between arrows.

C – Red Stocking
Side #2
(cut 1 from 7-count)
13 x 17 holes

Whipstitch

Whipstitch with red
between arrows.

D – Poinsettia Petal
(cut 2 from 10-count)
3 x 3 holes

E – Holly
(cut 1 from 10-count)
3 x 5 holes

Holly Berry

Poinsettia Assembly Illustration
(Pieces are shown in different
colors for clarity.)

D

D

Bead

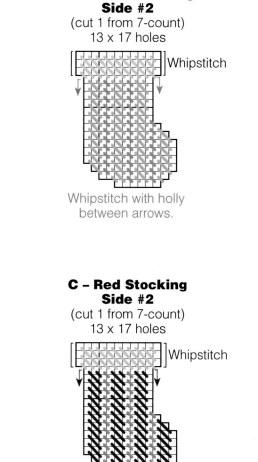

COLOR KEY: Festive Stockings

Metallic cord			AMOUNT
Yellow/Gold			4 yds. [3.7m]
White/Silver			2 yds. [1.8m]

Worsted-weight	Nylon Plus™	Need-loft®	YARN AMOUNT
Fern	#57	#23	7 yds. [6.4m]
Xmas Red	#19	#02	7 yds. [6.4m]
Sail Blue	#04	#35	6 yds. [5.5m]
White	#01	#41	6 yds. [5.5m]
Eggshell	#24	#39	4 yds. [3.7m]
Holly	#31	#27	2 yds. [1.8m]
Red	#20	#01	2 yds. [1.8m]
Royal	#09	#32	2 yds. [1.8m]

PLACEMENT KEY:

O Bead

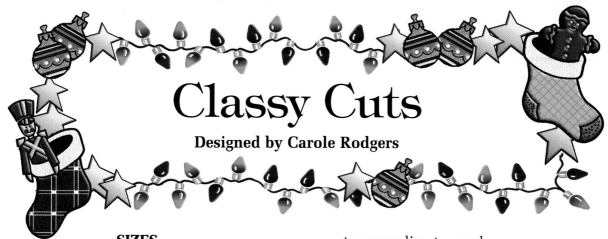

Classy Cuts

Designed by Carole Rodgers

SIZES

Angel is 2¾" x 2¾" [7cm x 7cm]; Frame and Santa are each 2¾" x 2¾" [5.7cm x 7cm], not including beard or pom-pom; Snowman is 2¼" x 2½" [5.7cm x 6.4cm]; Tree is 1⅞" x 3⅜" [4.8cm x 8.6cm], not including star.

SKILL LEVEL: Average

MATERIALS

❑ One Uniek® 5" [12.7cm] plastic canvas hexagon shape
❑ Two Uniek® 5" [12.7cm] plastic canvas star shapes
❑ Scraps of 7-count plastic canvas
❑ One white/silver tinsel ½" [13mm] and one red ¼" [6mm] pom-pom
❑ One red 14mm acrylic faceted star stone
❑ Craft glue or glue gun
❑ Six-strand embroidery floss; for amounts see Color Key on page 130.
❑ Metallic cord; for amounts see Color Key.
❑ Worsted weight or plastic canvas yarn; for amounts see Color Key.

CUTTING INSTRUCTIONS

NOTE: Graphs on pages 130 and 131.
A: For Angel body, cut one from hexagon according to graph.
B: For Angel arms, cut one from hexagon according to graph.
C: For Angel wings, cut one from one star according to graph.
D: For Angel head, cut one from 7-count according to graph.
E: For Frame front and backing, cut one each from one star according to graph.
F: For Santa front and backing, cut one each from one star according to graph.
G: For Santa hat brim, cut one from 7-count 2 x 16 holes.
H: For Snowman head, cut one from one star according to graph.
I: For Snowman bow, cut one from one star according to graph.
J: For Snowman holly leaves, cut two from one

star according to graph.
K: For Snowman hat brim, cut one from 7-count 2 x 14 holes.
L: For Tree, cut one from hexagon according to graph.
M: For Tree stand, cut one from hexagon according to graph.
N: For Tree trunk, cut one from 7-count 2 x 8 holes.

STITCHING INSTRUCTIONS

NOTE: One E for backing and one F for backing are not worked.
1: Using colors and stitches indicated, work A-D, one E for front, one F for front and G-N pieces according to graphs. With gold yarn for Angel's head as indicated on graph and with matching colors, Overcast cutout edges of front E and outer edges of A-D, and G-N pieces.
2: Using yarn and two strands floss in colors and embroidery stitches indicated, embroider facial detail on D, front F and H pieces as indicated.
3: For Angel, glue A-D pieces together as shown in photo.
NOTE: Cut one 9" [22.9cm] length of white/gold cord.
4: For Frame, with white/gold, Whipstitch indicated edges of front and backing E pieces together; Overcast unfinished front edges. Slide photo of choice between front and backing. Thread one end of strand from back to front through each ▲ hole as indicated; tie into a bow at front and trim ends.
5: For Santa, with red, Whipstitch hat edges of F pieces wrong sides together as indicated; with white, work Continuous Lark's Head Knots (See stitch illustration on page 130; leave 1" [2.5cm] tails.) through both thicknesses at ▲ holes as indicated. Fray ends to fluff. Glue tinsel pom-pom and hat brim to head as shown.
6: For Snowman, glue holly leaves, hat brim, bow and red pom-pom to head as shown.
7: For Tree, glue tree trunk to back of tree and tree stand as shown; glue star to tree top. ✳

Classy Cuts

Instructions and photo on pages 128 & 129

A – Angel Body
B – Angel Arms
L – Tree
M – Tree Stand
(cut 1 each from 1 hexagon)

Continuous Lark's Head Knot Stitch Illustration

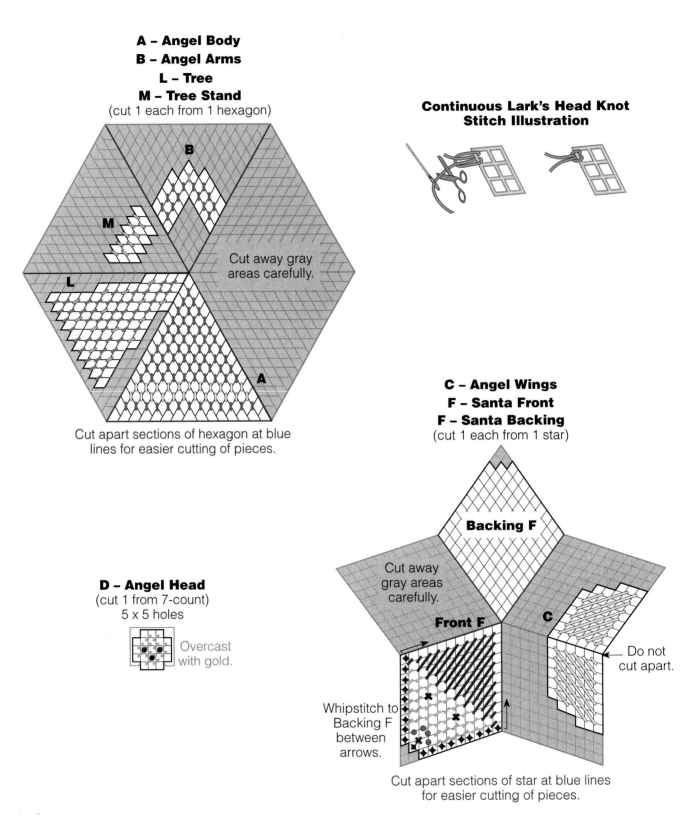

Cut away gray areas carefully.

Cut apart sections of hexagon at blue lines for easier cutting of pieces.

C – Angel Wings
F – Santa Front
F – Santa Backing
(cut 1 each from 1 star)

Backing F

Cut away gray areas carefully.

Front F

C

Do not cut apart.

Whipstitch to Backing F between arrows.

Cut apart sections of star at blue lines for easier cutting of pieces.

D – Angel Head
(cut 1 from 7-count)
5 x 5 holes

Overcast with gold.

E – Frame Front
E – Frame Backing
H – Snowman Head
I – Snowman Bow
(cut 1 each from 1 star)
J – Holly Leaf
(cut 2 from 1 star)

G – Santa Hat Brim
(cut 1 from 7-count) 2 x 16 holes

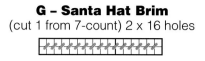

K – Snowman Hat Brim
(cut 1 from 7-count) 2 x 14 holes

N – Tree Trunk
(cut 1 from 7-count)
2 x 8 holes

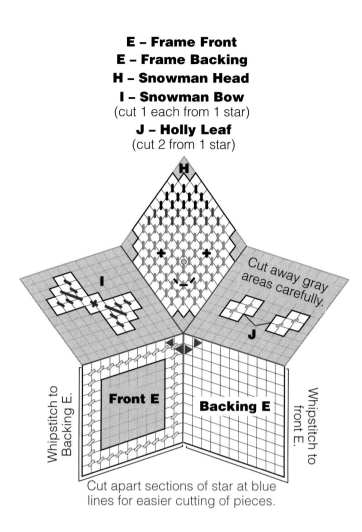

Cut away gray areas carefully.

Whipstitch to Backing E.

Front E

Backing E

Whipstitch to front E.

Cut apart sections of star at blue lines for easier cutting of pieces.

COLOR KEY: Classy Cuts

Embroidery floss			AMOUNT
■ Black			1/4 yd. [0.2m]
■ Red			1/4 yd. [0.2m]
Metallic cord			**AMOUNT**
◪ White/Gold			6 yds. [5.5m]
◪ Red			2 yds. [1.8m]

Worsted-weight	Nylon Plus™	Need-loft®	YARN AMOUNT
White	#01	#41	9 yds. [8.2m]
Red	#20	#01	5 yds. [4.6m]
Holly	#31	#27	4 yds. [3.7m]
Black	#02	#00	3 yds. [2.7m]
Baby Pink	#10	#08	2 yds. [1.8m]
Cinnamon	#44	#14	1/2 yd. [0.5m]
Pink	#11	#07	1/2 yd. [0.5m]
Gold	#27	#17	1/4 yd. [0.2m]

STITCH KEY:
– Backstitch/Straight
• French Knot
✦ Continuous Lark's Head Knot
▲ Frame Bow Attachment

Quick & Easy Bazaar

These petite projects offer super-sized rewards! Discover new ways to show-off your stitching talents with this lively exhibit of nifty ideas you can stitch in a hurry. Handy household helpers are always a hit, and fun fashion accessories let everyone put on the ritz. When you're looking for projects you can stitch in a few hours, the terrific patterns offered here will take first place on your list. When decorative do-dads are the order of the day, you're destined to win a blue ribbon for your outstanding stitching performance. Judge for yourself! These winning designs are just the thing to bring you "Best of Show."

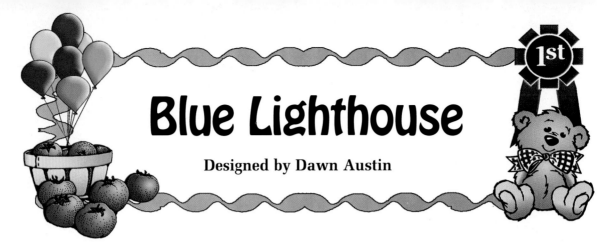

Blue Lighthouse

Designed by Dawn Austin

SIZE

4⅛" x 7⅛" [10.5cm x 18.1cm], not including hanger.

SKILL LEVEL: Average

MATERIALS

- ❑ One sheet of 7-count plastic canvas
- ❑ 1⅛" [2.9cm] suction cup with hook
- ❑ Six-strand embroidery floss; for amount see Color Key.
- ❑ Worsted weight or plastic canvas yarn; for amounts see Color Key.

CUTTING INSTRUCTIONS

For front and backing, cut two (one for front and one for backing) according to graph.

COLOR KEY: Blue Lighthouse

Embroidery floss			AMOUNT
■ Black			8 yds. [7.3m]
Worsted-weight	**Nylon Plus™**	**Need-loft®**	**YARN AMOUNT**
Black	#02	#00	7 yds. [6.4m]
Royal	#09	#32	5 yds. [4.6m]
Cinnamon	#44	#14	3 yds. [2.7m]
Forest	#32	#29	3 yds. [2.7m]
Pewter	#40	#65	3 yds. [2.7m]
Turquoise	#03	#54	3 yds. [2.7m]
White	#01	#41	3 yds. [2.7m]
Baby Blue	#05	#36	2 yds. [1.8m]
Beige	#43	#40	2 yds. [1.8m]
Mermaid Green	#37	#53	2 yds. [1.8m]
Yellow	#26	#57	1 yd. [0.9m]

STITCH KEY:

— Backstitch/Straight

STITCHING INSTRUCTIONS

NOTE: Backing is not worked.

1: Using colors and stitches indicated, work front according to graph; using yarn and six strands floss and Backstitch, embroider detail on front as indicated on graph.

2: Holding backing to wrong side of front, with black yarn, Whipstitch together.

3: Insert hook through upper cutout; hang or display as desired.❋

Front & Backing

(cut 1 each) 27 x 47 holes

Cut out gray areas carefully.

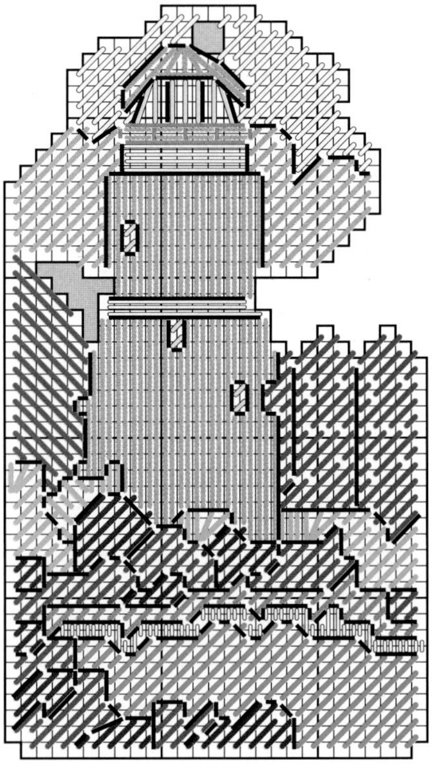

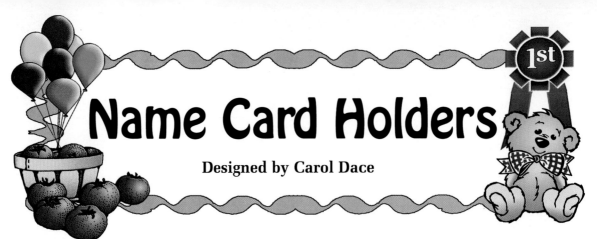

Name Card Holders

Designed by Carol Dace

SIZE

Each is 1⅛" x 1½" x 2¾" [2.9cm x 3.8cm x 7cm], not including name card.

SKILL LEVEL: Easy

MATERIALS FOR FOUR

❏ One sheet of 7-count plastic canvas
❏ 1⅓ yds. [1.2m] of gold ⅛" [3mm] metallic ribbon
❏ Four gold ⅜" [10mm] jingle bells
❏ Craft glue or glue gun
❏ Worsted weight or plastic canvas yarn; for amounts see Color Key.

CUTTING INSTRUCTIONS

A: For sides, cut eight according to graph.
B: For bottoms, cut four 7 x 18 holes.

STITCHING INSTRUCTIONS

1: Using colors and stitches indicated, work pieces according to graphs; with matching colors, Overcast edges of A pieces as indicated on graph.

2: For each Name Card Holder (make four), with violet and bending B to fit, Whipstitch two A and one B pieces wrong sides together ac-cording to Name Card Holder Assembly Illustration.

NOTE: Cut ribbon into four 12" [30.5cm] lengths.

3: Thread one bell onto each ribbon; tie each ribbon into a bow. Glue one bow to each Name Card Holder as shown in photo; trim bow ends as desired.✿

A – Side
(cut 8)
7 x 18 holes
Overcast
between arrows.

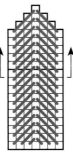

B – Bottom
(cut 4) 7 x 18 holes

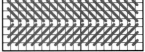

Name Card Holder Assembly Illustration

COLOR KEY: Name Card Holders

	Worsted-weight	Nylon Plus™	Need-loft®	YARN AMOUNT
■	Violet	#49	#04	32 yds. [29.3m]
■	Forest	#32	#29	7 yds. [6.4m]

Fright Fest

Designed by Kristine Loffredo

SIZES

Each Ghost is $1\frac{5}{8}$" x $2\frac{1}{4}$" [4.1cm x 5.7cm]; each Pumpkin is $1\frac{3}{8}$" x $1\frac{5}{8}$" [3.5cm x 4.1cm].

SKILL LEVEL: Easy

MATERIALS

- ❑ ½ sheet of 7-count plastic canvas
- ❑ ½ yd. [0.5m] of orange ⅛" [3mm] satin ribbon
- ❑ Four 17mm button covers
- ❑ One 3" [7.6cm] hair clip
- ❑ Craft glue or glue gun
- ❑ Worsted weight or plastic canvas yarn; for amounts see Color Key.

CUTTING INSTRUCTIONS

A: For Ghosts #1, cut two according to graph.
B: For Ghost #2, cut one according to graph.
C: For Pumpkins, cut four according to graph.

STITCHING INSTRUCTIONS

1: Using colors and stitches indicated, work pieces according to graphs; with matching colors, Overcast edges of pieces.
2: Using black (Separate into individual plies, if desired.) and French Knot, embroider detail on A and B pieces as indicated on graphs.
3: For barrette, glue one A and two C pieces to clip as shown in photo.
NOTE: Cut ribbon in half.
4: Fold each ribbon in half; overlap ribbon ends and leave an open loop. Glue one ribbon to wrong side of each remaining A and B (see photo).
5: Glue front of each button cover to wrong side of remaining pieces.✻

A – Ghost #1
(cut 2) 10 x 14 holes

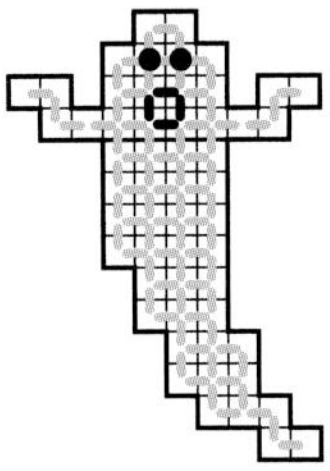

B – Ghost #2
(cut 1) 11 x 14 holes

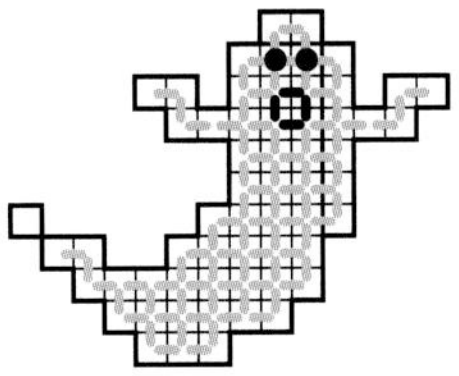

C – Pumpkin
(cut 4)
9 x 10 holes

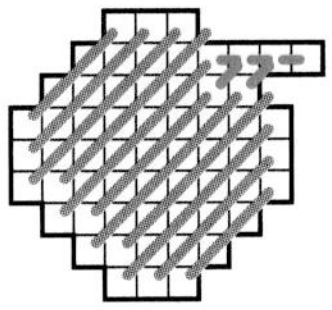

COLOR KEY: Fright Fest

Worsted-weight	Nylon Plus™	Need-loft®	YARN AMOUNT
White	#01	#41	8 yds. [7.3m]
Bright Orange	#17	#58	7 yds. [6.4m]
Holly	#31	#27	2 yds. [1.8m]
Black	#02	#00	1 yd. [0.9m]

STITCH KEY:
- ● French Knot

Scare up some fun with this "howl-ariously" cute barrette and button cover set.

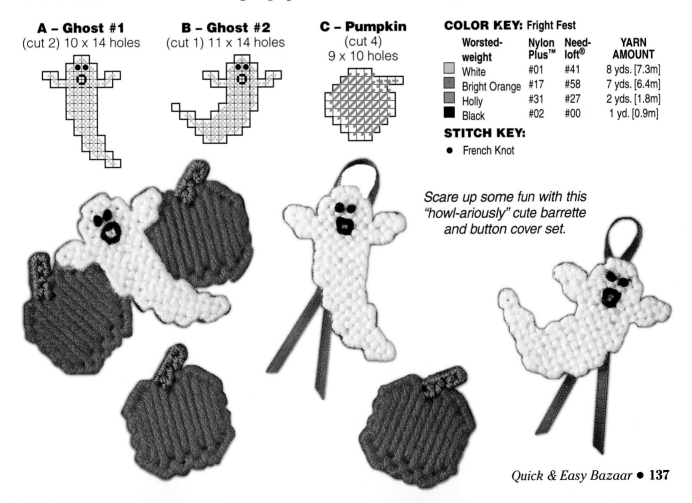

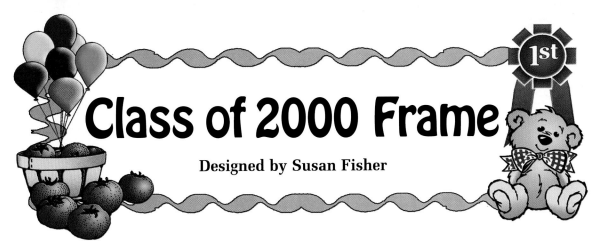

Class of 2000 Frame

Designed by Susan Fisher

SIZE
5⅜" x 15⅜" [13.7cm x 39.1cm] with three 1⅞" x 2¾" [4.8cm x 7cm] photo windows.

SKILL LEVEL: Easy

MATERIALS
- ❏ Two sheets of 7-count plastic canvas
- ❏ Craft glue or glue gun
- ❏ Worsted weight or plastic canvas yarn; for amounts see Color Key.

CUTTING INSTRUCTIONS
A: For "2" front and backing, cut two (one for front and one for backing) according to graph.

B: For "0" fronts and backings, cut six (three for fronts and three for backings) according to graph.

STITCHING INSTRUCTIONS
NOTE: Backing pieces are not worked.

1: Using main color and Continental Stitch, work front pieces; with contrasting color, Overcast cutout edges of front B pieces.

2: Using black and Backstitch, embroider detail on front A as indicated on graph.

3: Holding corresponding backing pieces to wrong sides of front pieces, Whipstitch front and backing pieces together and to adjacent pieces through all thicknesses according to Frame Assembly Illustration.✷

COLOR KEY: Class of 2000 Frame

Worsted-weight	YARN AMOUNT
☐ Main Color	30 yds. [27.4m]
☐ Contrasting Color	16 yds. [14.6m]
■ Black	3 yds. [2.7m]

STITCH KEY:
— Backstitch/Straight

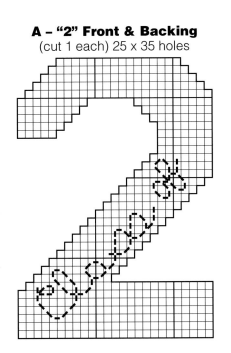

A – "2" Front & Backing
(cut 1 each) 25 x 35 holes

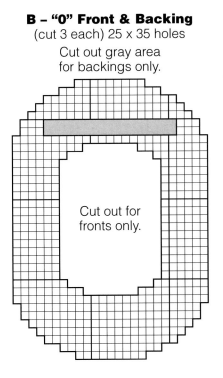

B – "0" Front & Backing
(cut 3 each) 25 x 35 holes
Cut out gray area for backings only.

Cut out for fronts only.

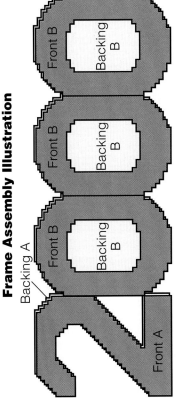

Frame Assembly Illustration

Front B — Backing B

Front B — Backing B

Front B — Backing B

Backing A

Front A

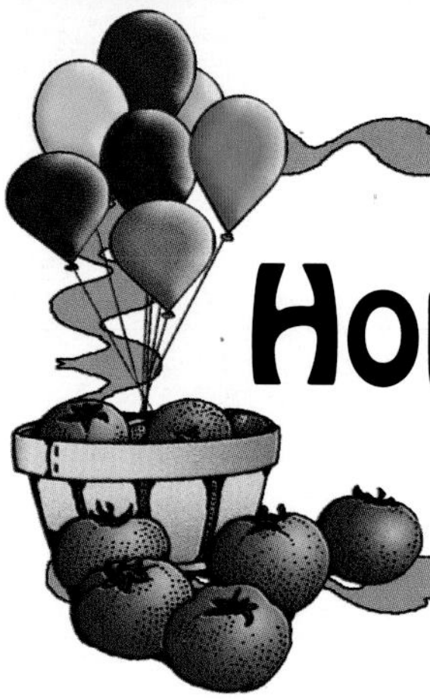

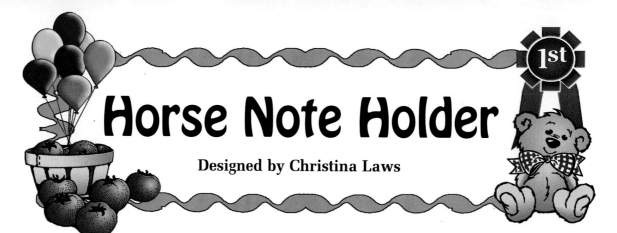

Horse Note Holder

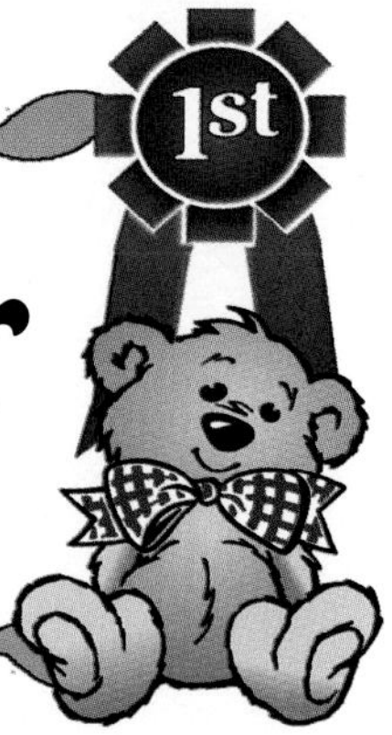

Designed by Christina Laws

SIZE

6½" x 7¾" [16.5cm x 19.7cm].

SKILL LEVEL: Average

MATERIALS

- ❑ 1½ sheets of 7-count plastic canvas
- ❑ Four clothespins
- ❑ Yellow and black craft paint
- ❑ 5" [12.7cm] piece of magnetic tape
- ❑ Craft glue or glue gun
- ❑ Worsted weight or plastic canvas yarn; for amounts see Color Key.

CUTTING INSTRUCTIONS

A: For heads, cut two according to graph.
B: For bodies, cut two according to graph.
C: For fence post pieces, cut four 4 x 29 holes (no graph).
D: For fence rail pieces, cut six 3 x 49 holes (no graph).

STITCHING INSTRUCTIONS

1: Using yellow and Continental Stitch, work A and B pieces; Overcast edges.
2: Using colors and embroidery stitches indicated, embroider detail on A pieces as indicated on graph, leaving ⅝" [16mm] tails on Lark's Head Knots for forelock.
3: Using red and stitches indicated, work C and D pieces according to stitch pattern guides.
4: For each fence post (make two), Whipstitch two C pieces wrong sides together.
5: For each fence rail (make three), Whipstitch two D pieces wrong sides together.
6: For legs, paint clothespins yellow; for hooves, paint bottoms black as shown in photo.
7: Glue pieces together according to Note Holder Assembly Illustration; glue two legs to each B as indicated.
8: Press adhesive side of magnetic tape to back side of top fence rail.✻

STITCH KEY:

- — Backstitch/Straight
- ● French Knot
- × Cross Stitch
- ◆ Lark's Head Knot
- ☐ Leg Placement

COLOR KEY: Horse Note Holder

	Worsted-weight	Nylon Plus™	Need-loft®	YARN AMOUNT
■	Red	#20	#01	30 yds. [27.4m]
☐	Yellow	#26	#57	25 yds. [22.9m]
■	White	#01	#41	3 yds. [2.7m]
■	Black	#02	#00	½ yd. [0.5m]

Note Holder Assembly Illustration

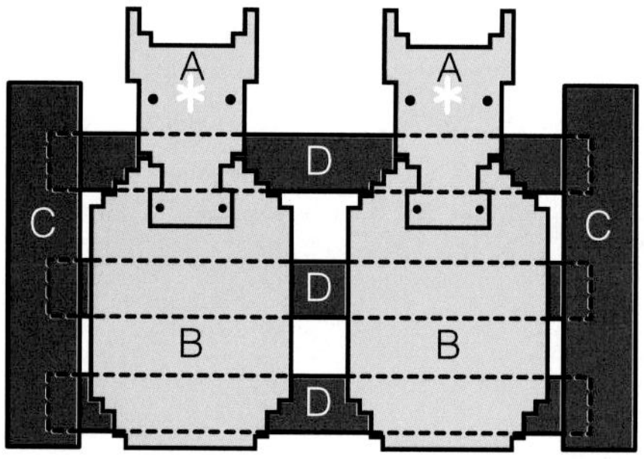

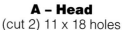

B – Body
(cut 2) 17 x 27 holes

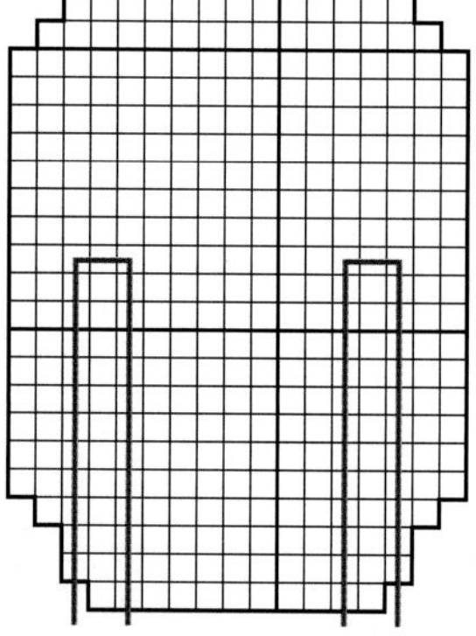

Fence Post Stitch Pattern Guide

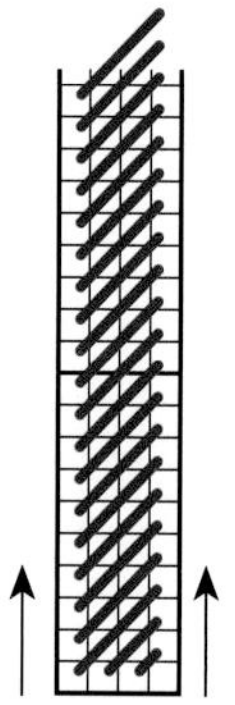

Continue established pattern across each entire piece.

A – Head
(cut 2) 11 x 18 holes

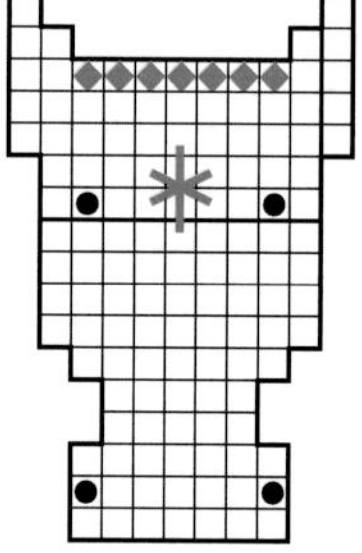

Fence Rail Stitch Pattern Guide

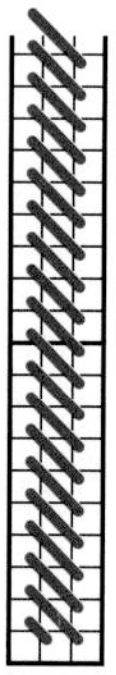

Continue established pattern across each entire piece.

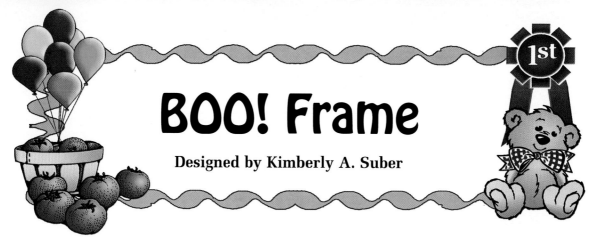

BOO! Frame

Designed by Kimberly A. Suber

SIZE
Frame is 5" x 5⅝" [12.7cm x 14.3cm] with a 2⅛" x 2¾" [5.4cm x 7cm] photo window. Measurements do not include pumpkin or moon.

SKILL LEVEL: Average

MATERIALS
❑ One sheet of 7-count plastic canvas
❑ Eight ⅝" [16mm] gold star spangles
❑ Craft glue or glue gun
❑ Worsted weight or plastic canvas yarn; for amounts see Color Key.

CUTTING INSTRUCTIONS
A: For front, cut one according to graph.
B: For back, cut one according to graph.
C: For stand, cut one 9 x 24 holes (no graph).
D: For pumpkin, cut one according to graph.
E: For pumpkin leaf, cut one according to graph.
F: For moon, cut one according to graph.
G: For bat, cut one according to graph.
H: For letters, cut one each according to graph.

STITCHING INSTRUCTIONS
NOTE: B and C pieces are not worked.
1: Using colors and stitches indicated, work A and D-G pieces according to graphs; with

holly for pumpkin stem and leaf, bittersweet for pumpkin, violet for letters and with matching colors, Overcast cutout edges of A and edges of D-H pieces.

2: Using black (Separate into individual plies, if desired.) and embroidery stitches indicated, embroider detail on letters as indicated on graph.

3: With royal, Whipstitch one end of stand to B as indicated; with stand to back, Whipstitch A and B pieces together.

4: Glue remaining pieces together and to Frame as shown in photo; glue stars to Frame as shown or as desired.✻

A – Front (cut 1) 33 x 37 holes

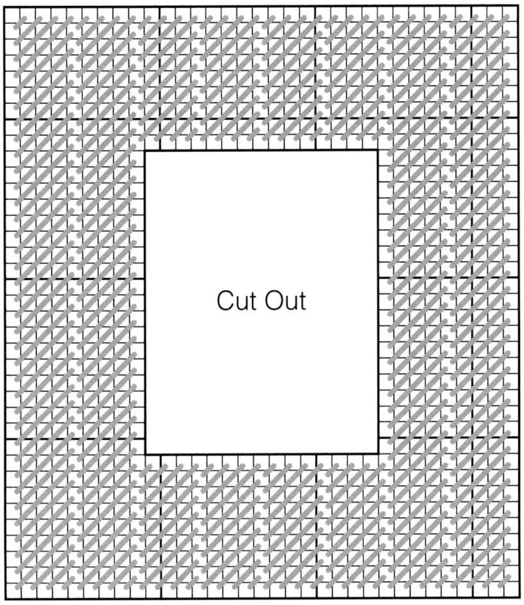

B – Back (cut 1) 33 x 37 holes
Cut out gray area.

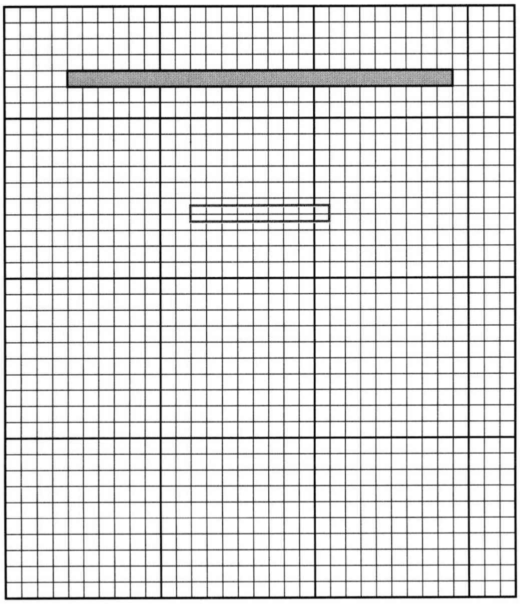

D – Pumpkin
(cut 1) 14 x 18 holes

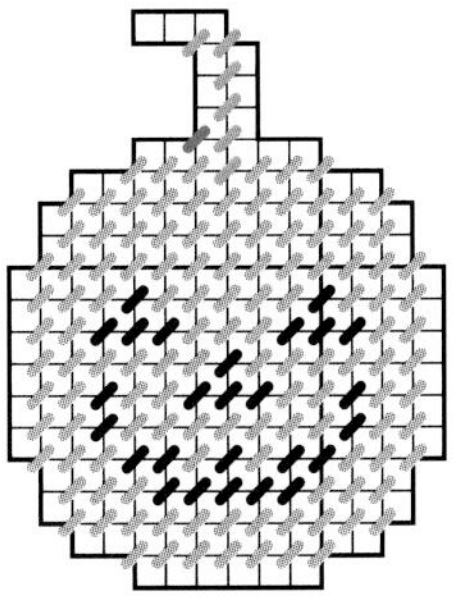

E – Pumpkin Leaf
(cut 1) 3 x 3 holes

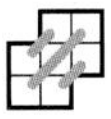

F – Moon
(cut 1)
14 x 14 holes

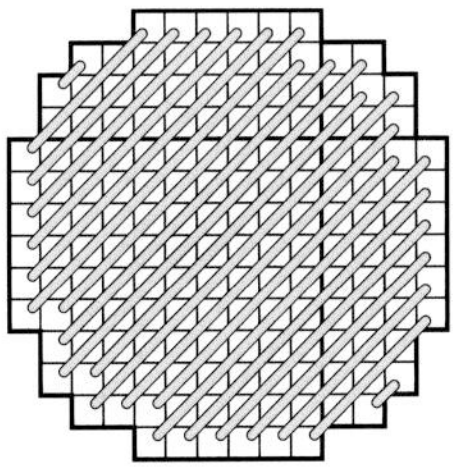

COLOR KEY: BOO! Frame

	Worsted-weight	Nylon Plus™	Need-loft®	YARN AMOUNT
▩	Royal	#09	#32	20 yds. [18.3m]
■	Black	#02	#00	6 yds. [5.5m]
▩	Bright Orange	#17	#58	4 yds. [3.7m]
□	Violet	#49	#04	4 yds. [3.7m]
▨	Yellow	#26	#57	4 yds. [3.7m]
□	Bittersweet	#18	#52	2 yds. [1.8m]
▩	Fern	#57	#23	1/2 yd. [0.5m]
▩	Holly	#31	#27	1/2 yd. [0.5m]

STITCH KEY:

— Backstitch/Straight
● French Knot
□ Stand Attachment

G – Bat
(cut 1)
6 x 13 holes

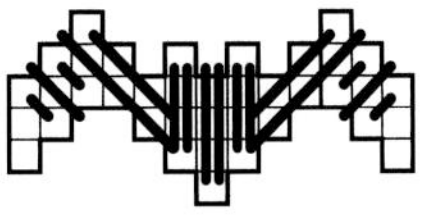

H – Letters (cut 1 each)

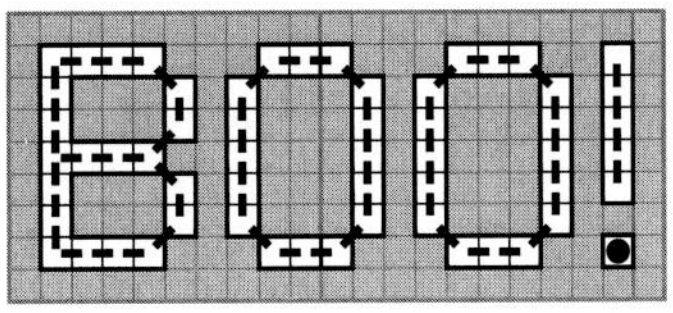

Towel Toppers

Designed by Jeannette Osborne

SIZES

Toppers #1 and #2 are 7⅛" across x 5¾"
[18.1cm x 14.6cm]; Topper #3 is 6¾" across x
5¼" [17.1cm x 13.3cm]. Measurements were
taken with hangers buttoned and do not
include laces or towels.

SKILL LEVEL: Average

MATERIALS

- ❑ One sheet each of Christmas green, teal and light blue 7-count plastic canvas
- ❑ Three standard-size kitchen towels of choice
- ❑ Sewing machine, serger or pinking shears
- ❑ 10" [25.4cm] of white/iridescent 1" [2.5cm] pre-gathered lace
- ❑ 20" [50.8cm] of white 1" [2.5cm] pre-gathered lace
- ❑ One red and one clear ½" [13mm] button
- ❑ One white ⅜" [10mm] button
- ❑ Four small silk flowers and leaves of choice
- ❑ Sewing needle and dark green and blue sewing thread
- ❑ 20" [50.8cm] of white ¾" [19mm] Velcro® Sew-On Strips
- ❑ Craft glue or glue gun
- ❑ Six-strand embroidery floss; for amount see Color Key on page 146.
- ❑ Worsted weight or plastic canvas yarn; for amounts see Color Key.

CUTTING INSTRUCTIONS

NOTE: See graphs for canvas colors.
For Towel Toppers #1-#3, cut one each according to graphs on pages 146 and 147.

STITCHING INSTRUCTIONS

1: Using colors and stitches indicated and leaving uncoded areas unworked, work pieces according to graphs; with matching colors, Overcast (Use Crossed Overcast for each hanger, if desired.) edges of pieces.

2: Using yarn and six strands floss in colors and embroidery stitches indicated, embroider detail on Toppers #2 and #3 as indicated on graphs.

NOTE: Cut each towel in half cross-wise.

3: To prevent unraveling, finish raw edge of each towel using matching color thread and a zig-zag stitch on sewing machine or serger, or cut with pinking shears.

NOTE: Cut Velcro® into three equal lengths.

4: Using sewing needle and dark green thread, sew red button to Topper #1 and clear button to Topper #2 as indicated; using blue thread, sew white button to Topper #3 as indicated.

5: With dark green thread, sew one towel, white/iridescent lace, one piece of Velcro® and Topper #1 together according to Towel Topper Assembly Diagram.

NOTE: Cut white lace in half.

6: For Toppers #2 and #3, repeat Step 5 with remaining pieces, substituting blue thread for green thread on Topper #3 and white lace for white/iridescent lace for both.

7: Glue leaves and flowers to Topper #1 as shown in photo or as desired.✤

Towel Toppers

Instructions and photo on pages 144 & 145

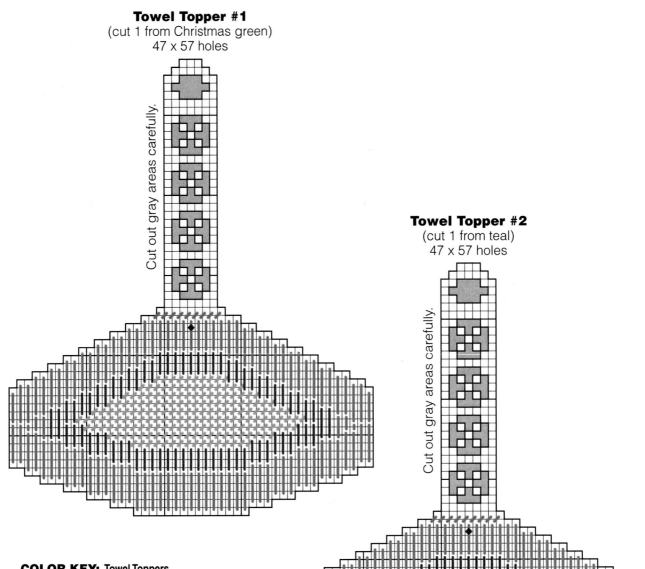

Towel Topper #1
(cut 1 from Christmas green)
47 x 57 holes

Cut out gray areas carefully.

Towel Topper #2
(cut 1 from teal)
47 x 57 holes

Cut out gray areas carefully.

COLOR KEY: Towel Toppers

Embroidery floss			AMOUNT
Green			6 yds. [5.5m]

Worsted-weight	Nylon Plus™	Need-loft®	YARN AMOUNT
Forest	#32	#29	30 yds. [27.4m]
Red	#20	#01	18 yds. [16.5m]
Royal	#09	#32	15 yds. [13.7m]
Fern	#57	#23	4 yds. [3.7m]
Sail Blue	#04	#35	4 yds. [3.7m]
Yellow	#26	#57	4 yds. [3.7m]

STITCH KEY:

— Backstitch/Straight

◦ Lazy Daisy

◆ Button Attachment

Towel Topper Assembly Diagram

Step 1:
Separate sides of Velcro®; sew lace and one side of Velcro® to bottom edge of towel topper.

Step 3:
Run a basting stitch across cut edge of towel; slightly gather towel edge to fit across top of Towel Topper.

Step 4:
To hold gathers, pin remaining Velcro® side over top edge of towel; sew over Velcro® and remove basting stitches.

Step 5:
Remove pins; press Velcro® side pieces together.

Step 2:
Trim away excess lace and Velcro®; fold under lace ends and tack in place.

Towel Topper #3
(cut 1 from light blue)
45 x 47 holes

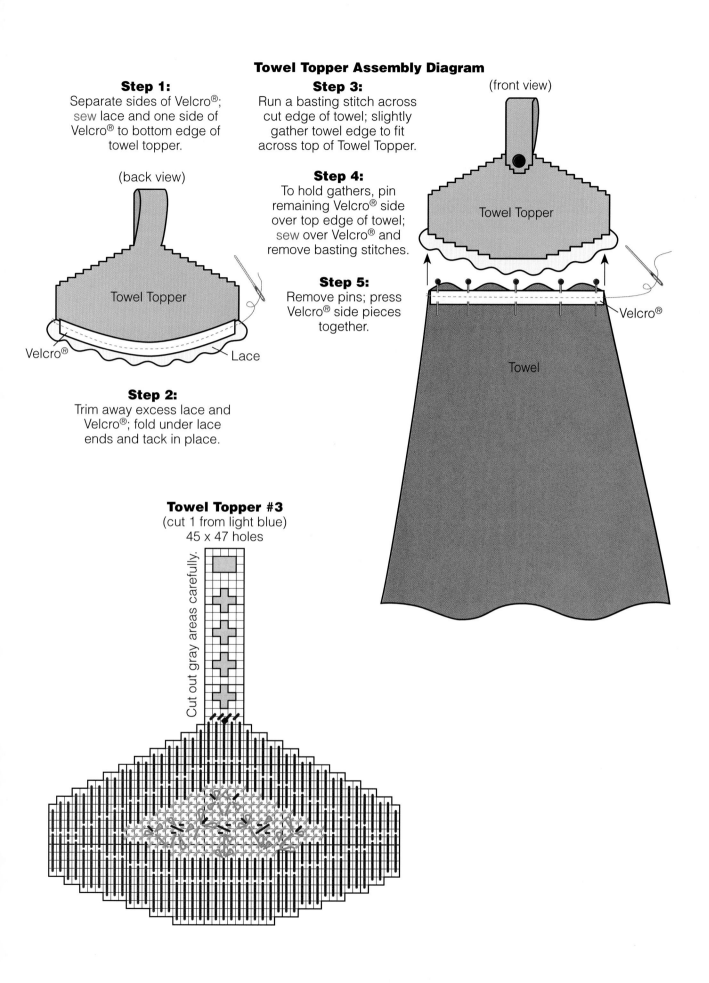

(back view)

Towel Topper

Velcro®

Lace

(front view)

Towel Topper

Velcro®

Towel

Cut out gray areas carefully.

These "corny" magnet pals will have everyone crowing with delight over your stitching talents.

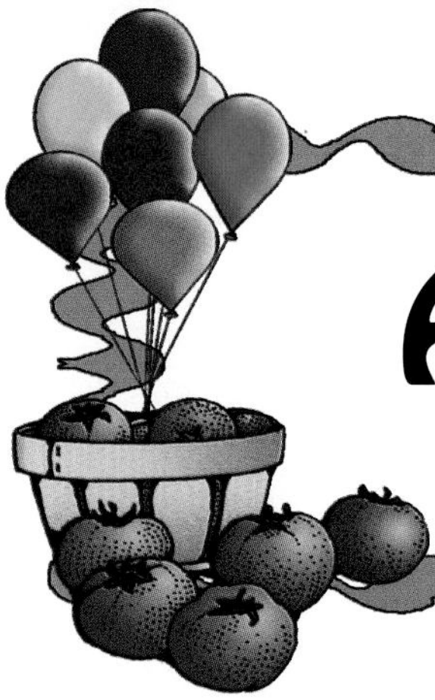

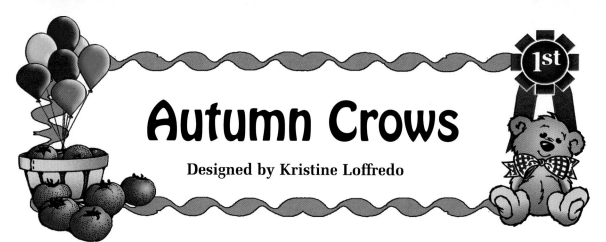

Autumn Crows

Designed by Kristine Loffredo

SIZES

Pumpkin Crow is 4" x 3⅝" [10.2cm x 9.2cm];
Acorn Crow is 4" x 4" [10.2cm x 10.2cm].

SKILL LEVEL: Easy

MATERIALS

- ❑ One sheet of 7-count plastic canvas
- ❑ 4" [10.2cm] piece of magnetic tape
- ❑ Craft glue or glue gun
- ❑ Worsted weight or plastic canvas yarn; for amounts see Color Key.

CUTTING INSTRUCTIONS

A: For acorn and pumpkin Crows, cut one each according to graphs.
B: For beaks, cut two according to graphs.
C: For gold and green leaves, cut two each according to graphs.
D: For corn, cut two according to graph.
E: For acorns, cut two according to graph.
F: For acorn crowns, cut two according to graph.

STITCHING INSTRUCTIONS

1: Using colors and stitches indicated, work pieces (one of each C and one F on opposite side of canvas) according to graphs; with matching colors, Overcast edges.
2: Using black (Separate into individual plies, if desired.) and embroidery stitches indicated, embroider detail on A pieces as indicated on graphs.
3: For each Crow, with black, tack one beak to each A as indicated; glue one D under each beak.
4: For acorn Crow, glue acorn A, gold C pieces, E and F pieces together as shown in photo; for pumpkin Crow, glue right side of green C pieces to wrong side of pumpkin A as shown.
NOTE: Cut magnetic tape into four 1" [2.5cm] pieces.
5: Glue one magnetic strip to wrong side of each leaf.✻

A – Pumpkin Crow
(cut 1) 18 x 18 holes

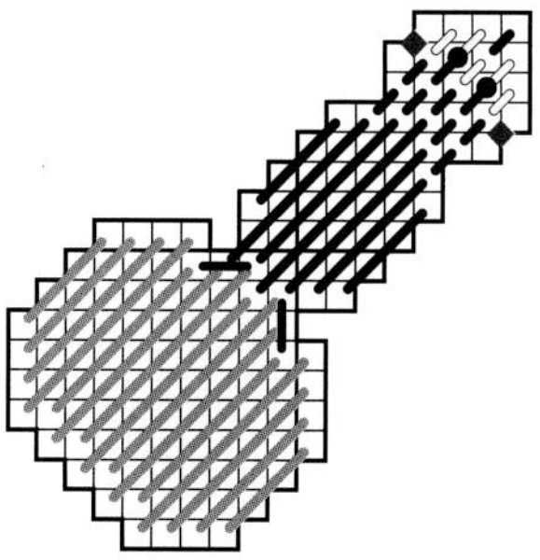

A – Acorn Crow
(cut 1) 16 x 16 holes

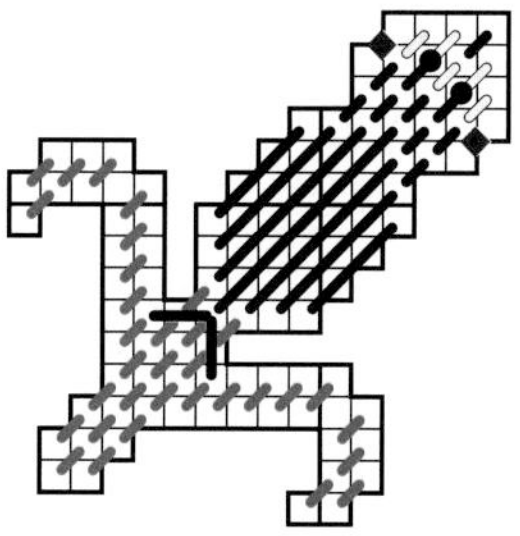

B – Beak
(cut 2)
4 x 4 holes

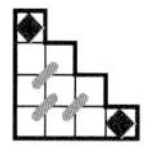

D – Corn
(cut 2)
5 x 5 holes

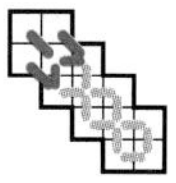

C – Gold Leaf
(cut 2) 12 x 18 holes

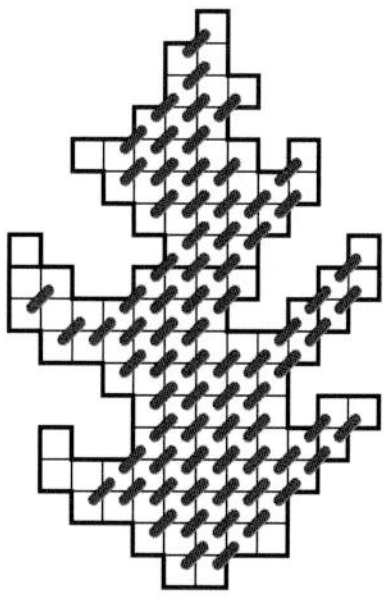

C – Green Leaf
(cut 2) 10 x 18 holes

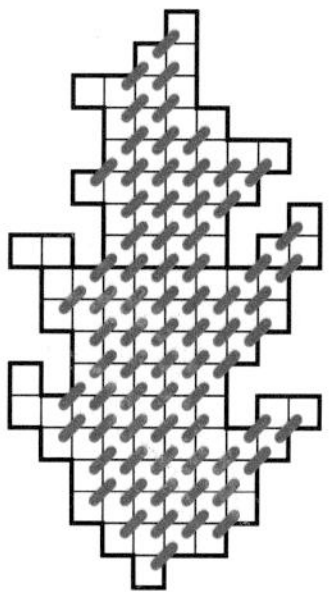

COLOR KEY: Autumn Crow Magnets

Worsted-weight	Nylon Plus™	Need-loft®	YARN AMOUNT
Holly	#31	#27	10 yds. [9.1m]
Gold	#27	#17	7 yds. [6.4m]
Black	#02	#00	6 yds. [5.5m]
Bittersweet	#18	#52	3 yds. [2.7m]
Brown	#36	#15	3 yds. [2.7m]
Baby Yellow	#42	#21	2 yds. [1.8m]
Sandstone	#47	#16	2 yds. [1.8m]
Yellow	#26	#57	2 yds. [1.8m]
White	#01	#41	1/2 yd. [0.5m]

STITCH KEY:
- — Backstitch/Straight
- ● French Knot
- ◆ Beak Attachment

E – Acorn
(cut 2)
5 x 5 holes

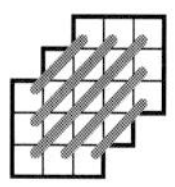

F – Acorn Crown
(cut 2) 5 x 7 holes

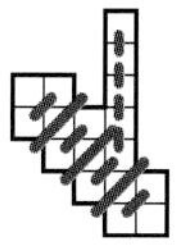

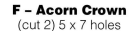

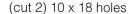

Buggy
Pin Pals

Leave a
Note

Buggy Pin Pals

Designed by Joyce Keklock

SIZES

Ladybug is ¾" x ¾" [1.9cm x 1.9cm]; Bee is ⅝" x 1" [1.6cm x 2.5cm]; Dragonfly is ¾" x 1¾" [0.6cm x 3.2cm]; Butterfly is 1" x ⅞" [2.5cm x 2.2cm]. Measurements do not include antennae or wings.

SKILL LEVEL: Easy

MATERIALS

- ❑ ¼ sheet of 10-count plastic canvas
- ❑ Six 3mm wiggle eyes
- ❑ Four 10mm tie tacks with 4mm pads
- ❑ Craft glue or glue gun
- ❑ Six-strand embroidery floss; for amounts see Color Key.

CUTTING INSTRUCTIONS

NOTE: Graphs on page 152.
A: For Ladybug, cut one according to graph.
B: For Bee, cut one according to graph.
C: For Dragonfly, cut one according to graph.
D: For Butterfly, cut one according to graph.

STITCHING INSTRUCTIONS

1: Using 12 strands floss in colors indicated and Continental Stitch, work pieces according to graphs; with green for Dragonfly, black for Butterfly and with matching colors, Overcast edges.
2: Using three strands black floss and embroidery stitches indicated, embroider detail on

Continued on page 152

Leave A Note

Designed by Sandra Miller Maxfield

SIZE

5½" x 6⅛" [14cm x 15.6cm], not including note pad.

SKILL LEVEL: Average

MATERIALS

- ❑ One sheet of 7-count plastic canvas
- ❑ 5½" [14cm] of paper-covered 18-gauge wire
- ❑ 3" x 5" [7.6cm x 12.7cm] bottom-opening note pad
- ❑ Craft glue or glue gun
- ❑ Worsted weight or plastic canvas yarn; for amounts see Color Key.

CUTTING INSTRUCTIONS

NOTE: Graphs on page 153.
A: For note holder, cut one according to graph.
B: For bird, cut one according to graph.
C: For flowers, cut three according to graph.
D: For leaves, cut three according to graph.
E: For pencil holder, cut one 1 x 13 holes (no graph).

STITCHING INSTRUCTIONS

1: Using colors and stitches indicated, work A-D pieces according to graphs; with baby blue for E and with matching colors, Overcast edges of pieces.

Continued on page 153

Buggy Pin Pals

Continued from page 151

A and B pieces as indicated on graphs.
3: For each pair of antennae, using three strands black floss, knot end of thread; take one small stitch on wrong side at top of Ladybug, Bee and Butterfly head, pulling ends to even at desired lengths. Knot remaining floss end; cut away excess floss.
4: For Bee and Dragonfly wings, using six strands white floss for Bee and six strands light gold floss for Dragonfly, beginning and ending each loop in indicated holes, make two desired-length loops.
5: Glue two wiggle eyes to each Ladybug, Bee and Dragonfly; glue one tack pad to wrong side of each Bug.❖

A – Ladybug
(cut 1) 6 x 7 holes

B – Bee
(cut 1)
7 x 7 holes

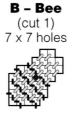

C – Dragonfly
(cut 1) 8 x 8 holes

D – Butterfly
(cut 1) 8 x 8 holes

COLOR KEY: Buggy Pin Pals

Embroidery floss		AMOUNT
■	Black	4 yds. [3.7m]
▨	Orange	2 yds. [1.8m]
■	Red	2 yds. [1.8m]
▨	Yellow	2 yds. [1.8m]
▨	Green	1 yd. [0.9m]
□	Light Gold	½ yd. [0.5m]
□	White	½ yd. [0.5m]

STITCH KEY:
— Backstitch/Straight
● French Knot
◆ Wing Attachment

Try This!

Let your imagination soar. Use these cute little pin pals to lift your child's day. Dress up socks, a collar, or make a backpack uniquely theirs.

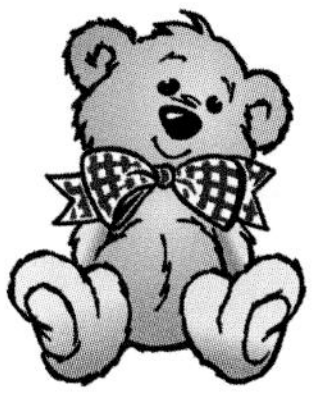

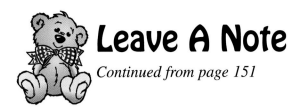

Leave A Note

Continued from page 151

2: Using black (Separate into individual plies, if desired.) and Backstitch, embroider detail on A as indicated on graph.

3: For pen holder, with baby blue, Whipstitch short edges of E together and tack to A as indicated.

NOTE: Cut wire into one 2" [5.1cm] and one 3½" [8.9cm] piece, forming branches.

4: For bird's feet, starting 1" [2.5cm] from one end of longer branch, wrap yellow yarn around branch about 4-5 times, covering a ½" [13mm] area; secure ends under wraps.

5: Bend branches to shape and glue to A as indicated, making sure bird's feet are in place as shown in photo.

6: Glue bird over feet as shown; glue one leaf and one flower over each branch end and to top left corner of holder. Hang as desired.✻

A – Note Holder
(cut 1) 25 x 40 holes

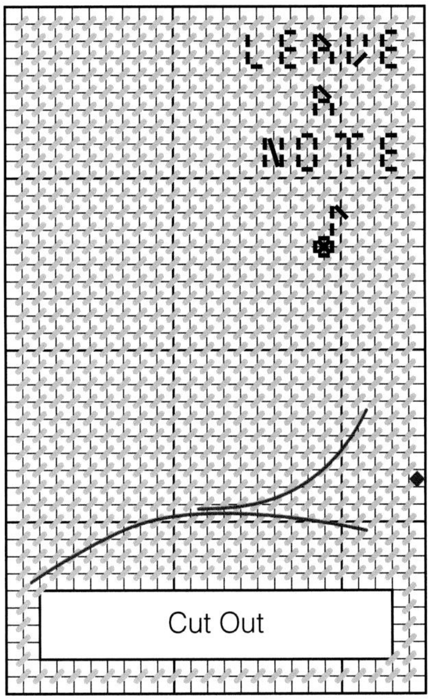

B – Bird
(cut 1)
20 x 22 holes

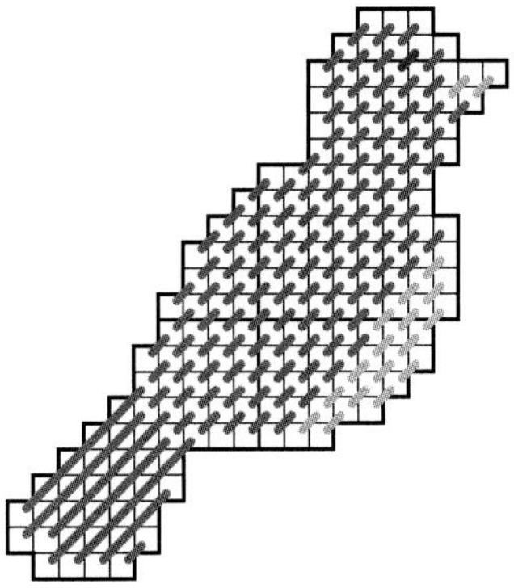

C – Flower
(cut 3)
7 x 7 holes

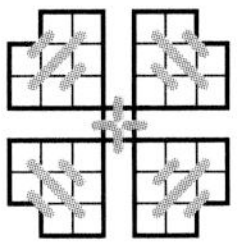

D – Leaf
(cut 3)
4 x 4 holes

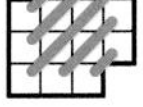

COLOR KEY: Leave A Note

Worsted-weight	Nylon Plus™	Need-loft®	YARN AMOUNT
Baby Blue	#13	#03	22 yds. [20.1m]
Cinnamon	#09	#32	6 yds. [5.5m]
Lavender	#35	#13	4 yds. [3.7m]
Holly	#04	#35	2 yds. [1.8m]
Yellow	#41	#19	1½ yds. [1.4m]
Sail Blue	#04	#35	¼ yd. [0.2m]

STITCH KEY:
- Backstitch/Straight
- ◆ Pen Holder Attachment
- Branch Placement

~General Instructions~

BASIC INSTRUCTIONS TO GET YOU STARTED

Most plastic canvas stitchers love getting their projects organized before they even step out the door in search of supplies. A few moments of careful planning can make the creation of your project even more fun.

First of all, prepare your work area. You will need a flat surface for cutting and assembly, and you will need a place to store your materials. Good lighting is essential, and a comfortable chair will make your stitching time even more enjoyable.

Do you plan to make one project, or will you be making several of the same item? A materials list appears at the beginning of each pattern. If you plan to make several of the same item, multiply your materials accordingly. Your shopping list is ready.

CANVAS

Most projects can be made using standard-size sheets of canvas. Standard-size sheets of 7-count (7 holes per inch) are always 70 x 90 holes and are about 10½" x 13½". For larger projects, 7-count canvas also comes in 12" x 18" (80 x 120 holes) and 13½" x 22½" (90 x 150 holes) sheets. Other shapes are available in 7-count, including circles, diamonds, purse forms and ovals.

10-count canvas (10 holes per inch) comes only in standard-size sheets, which vary slightly depending on brand. They are 10½" x 13½" (106 x 136 holes) or 11" x 14" (108 x 138 holes).

5-count canvas (5 holes per inch) and 14-count (14 holes per inch) sheets are also available.

Some canvas is soft and pliable, while other canvas is stiffer and more rigid. To prevent canvas from cracking during or after stitching, you'll want to choose pliable canvas for projects that require shaping, like round baskets with curved handles. For easier shaping, warm canvas pieces with a blow-dry hair dryer to soften; dip in cool water to set. If your project is a box or an item that will stand alone, stiffer canvas is more suitable.

Both 7- and 10-count canvas sheets are available in a rainbow of colors. Most designs can be stitched on colored as well as clear canvas. When a pattern does not specify color in the materials list, you can assume clear canvas was used in the photographed model. If you'd like to stitch only a portion of the design, leaving a portion unstitched, use colored canvas to coordinate with yarn colors.

Buy the same brand of canvas for each entire project. Different brands of canvas may differ slightly in the distance between each bar.

MARKING & COUNTING TOOLS

To avoid wasting canvas, careful cutting of each piece is important. For some pieces with square corners, you might be comfortable cutting the canvas without marking it beforehand. But for pieces with lots of angles and cutouts, you may want to mark your canvas before cutting.

Always count before you mark and cut. To count holes on the graphs, look for the bolder lines showing each ten holes. These ten-count lines begin in the lower left-hand corner of each graph and are on the graph to make counting easier. To count holes on the canvas, you may use your tapestry needle, a toothpick or a plastic hair roller pick. Insert the needle or pick slightly in each hole as you count.

Most stitchers have tried a variety of marking tools and have settled on a favorite, which may be crayon, permanent marker, grease pencil or ball point pen. One of the best marking tools is a fine-point overhead projection marker, available at office supply stores. The ink is dark and easy to see and washes off completely with water. After cutting and before stitching, it's important to remove all marks so they won't stain yarn as you stitch or show through stitches later. Cloth and paper toweling removes grease pencil and crayon marks, as do fabric softener sheets that have already been used in your dryer.

SUPPLIES

Yarn, canvas, needles, cutters and most other supplies needed to complete the projects in this book are available at craft and needlework stores and through mail order catalogs. Other supplies are available at fabric, hardware and discount stores.

YARN AND OTHER STITCHING MATERIALS

You may choose two-ply nylon plastic canvas yarn (the color numbers of two popular brands are found in the general materials lists and Color Keys) or four-ply worsted-weight yarn for stitching on 7-count canvas. There are about 42 yards per ounce of plastic canvas yarn and 50 yards per ounce of worsted-weight yarn.

Worsted-weight yarn is widely available and comes in wool, acrylic, cotton and blends. If you decide to use worsted-weight yarn, choose 100% acrylic for best coverage. Select worsted-weight yarn by color instead of the color names or numbers found in the Color Keys. Projects stitched with worsted-weight yarn often "fuzz" after use. "Fuzz" can be removed by shaving it off with a fabric shaver to make your project look new again.

Plastic canvas yarn comes in about 60 colors and is a favorite of many plastic canvas designers. These yarns "wear" well both while stitching and in the finished product. When buying plastic canvas yarn, shop using the color names or numbers found in the Color Keys, or select colors of your choice.

To cover 5-count canvas, use a doubled strand of worsted-weight or plastic canvas yarn.

Choose sport-weight yarn or #3 pearl cotton for stitching on 10-count canvas. To cover 10-count canvas using six-strand embroidery floss, use 12 strands held together. Single and double plies of yarn will also cover 10-count and can be used for embroidery or accent stitching worked over needlepoint stitches – simply separate worsted-weight yarn into 2-ply or plastic canvas yarn into 1-ply. Nylon plastic canvas yarn does not perform as well as knitting worsted when separated and can be frustrating to use, but it is possible. Just use short lengths, separate into single plies and twist each ply slightly.

Embroidery floss or #5 pearl cotton can also be used for embroidery, and each covers 14-count canvas well.

Metallic cord is a tightly-woven cord that comes in dozens of glittering colors. Some are solid-color metallics, including gold and silver, and some have colors interwoven with gold or silver threads. If your metallic cord has a white core, the core may be removed for super-easy stitching. To do so, cut a length of cord; grasp center core fibers with tweezers or fingertips and pull. Core slips out easily. Though the sparkly look of metallics will add much to your project, you may substitute contrasting colors of yarn.

Natural and synthetic raffia straw will cover 7-count canvas if flattened before stitching. Use short lengths to prevent splitting, and glue ends to prevent unraveling.

CUTTING CANVAS

Follow all Cutting Instructions, Notes and labels above graphs to cut canvas. Each piece is labeled with a letter of the alphabet. Square-sided pieces are cut according to hole count, and some may not have a graph.

Unlike sewing patterns, graphs are not designed to be used as actual patterns but rather as counting, cutting and stitching guides. Therefore, graphs may not be actual size. Count the holes on the graph (see Marking & Counting Tools on page 154), mark your canvas to match, then cut. The old carpenters' adage – "Measure twice, cut once" – is good advice. Trim off the nubs close to the bar, and trim all corners diagonally.

For large projects, as you cut each piece, it is a good idea to label it with its letter and name. Use sticky labels, or fasten scrap paper notes through the canvas with a twist tie or a quick stitch with a scrap of yarn. To stay organized, you many want to store corresponding pieces together in zip-close bags.

If you want to make several of a favorite design to give as gifts or sell at bazaars, make cutting canvas easier and faster by making a master pattern. From colored canvas, cut out one of each piece required. For duplicates, place the colored canvas on top of clear canvas and cut out. If needed, secure the canvas pieces together with paper fasteners, twist ties or yarn. By using this method, you only have to count from the graphs once.

If you accidentally cut or tear a bar or two on your canvas, don't worry! Boo-boos can usually be repaired in one of several ways: heat the tip of a metal skewer and melt the canvas back together; glue torn bars with a tiny drop of craft glue, super glue or hot glue; or reinforce the torn section with a separate piece of canvas placed at the back of your work. When reinforcing with extra canvas, stitch through both thicknesses.

Needles & Other Stitching Tools

Blunt-end tapestry needles are used for stitching plastic canvas. Choose a No. 16 needle for stitching 5- and 7-count, a No. 18 for stitching 10-count and a No. 24 for stitching 14-count canvas. A small pair of embroidery scissors for snipping yarn is handy. Try using needle-nosed jewelry pliers for pulling the needle through several thicknesses of canvas and out of tight spots too small for your hand.

Stitching the Canvas

Stitching Instructions for each section are found after the Cutting Instructions. First, refer to the illustrations of basic stitches found on page 157 to familiarize yourself with the stitches used. Illustrations will be found near the graphs for pieces worked using special stitches. Follow the numbers on the tiny graph beside the illustration to make each stitch – bring your needle up from the back of the work on odd numbers and down through the front of the work on the even numbers.

Before beginning, read the Stitching Instructions to get an overview of what you'll be doing. You'll find that some pieces are stitched using colors and stitches indicated on graphs, and for other pieces you will be given a color and stitch to use to cover the entire piece.

Cut yarn lengths between 18" to 36". Thread needle; do not tie a knot in the end. Bring your needle up through the canvas from the back, leaving a short length of yarn on the wrong side of the canvas. As you begin to stitch, work over this short length of yarn. If you are beginning with Continental Stitches, leave a 1" length, but if you are working longer stitches, leave a longer length.

In order for graph colors to contrast well, graph colors may not match yarn colors. For instance, a light yellow may be selected to represent the metallic cord color gold, or a light blue may represent white yarn.

When following a graph showing several colors, you may want to work all the stitches of one color at the same time. Some stitchers prefer to work with several colors at once by threading each on a separate needle and letting the yarn not being used hang on the wrong side of the work. Either way, remember that strands of yarn run across the wrong side of the work may show through the stitches from the front.

As you stitch, try to maintain an even tension on the yarn. Loose stitches will look uneven, and tight stitches will let the canvas show through. If your yarn twists as you work, you may want to let your needle and yarn hang and untwist occasionally.

When you end a section of stitching or finish a thread, weave the yarn through the back side of your last few stitches, then trim it off.

Construction & Assembly

After all pieces of an item needing assembly are stitched, you will find the order of assembly is listed in the Stitching Instructions and sometimes illustrated in Diagrams found with the graphs. For best results, join pieces in the order written. Refer to the Stitch Key and to the directives near the graphs for precise attachments.

Finishing Tips

To combat glue strings when using a hot glue gun, practice a swirling motion as you work. After placing the drop of glue on your work, lift the gun slightly and swirl to break the stream of glue, as if you were making an ice cream cone. Have a cup of water handy when gluing. For those times that you'll need to touch the glue, first dip your finger into the water just enough to dampen it. This will minimize the glue sticking to your finger, and it will cool and set the glue more quickly.

To attach beads, use a bit more glue to form a cup around the bead. If too much shows after drying, use a craft knife to trim off excess glue.

Scotchguard® or other fabric protectors may be used on your finished projects. However, avoid using a permanent marker if you plan to use a fabric protector, and be sure to remove all other markings before stitching. Fabric protectors can cause markings to bleed, staining yarn.

For More Information

Sometimes even the most experienced needlecrafters can find themselves having trouble following instructions. If you have difficulty completing your project, write to Plastic Canvas Editors, *The Needlecraft Shop*, 23 Old Pecan Road, Big Sandy, Texas 75755 (903) 636-4000 or (800) 259-4000, www.needlecraftshop.com.

~Stitch Guide~

NEEDLEPOINT STITCHES

CONTINENTAL
can be used to stitch designs or fill in background areas.

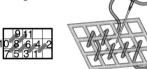

LONG
is a horizontal or vertical stitch used to stitch designs or fill in background areas. Can be stitched over two or more bars.

REVERSE CONTINENTAL
can be used to stitch designs or fill in background areas.

SCOTCH
is used to fill in background areas. Stitches cover a square area over three or more bars.

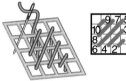

SLANTED GOBELIN
can be used to stitch designs or fill in background areas. Can be stitched over two or more bars in vertical or horizontal rows.

SMYRNA CROSS
can be used as a needlepoint stitch or as an embroidery stitch, stitched over background stitches with contrasting yarn or floss.

OVERCAST
is used to finish edges. Stitch two or three times in corners for complete coverage.

WHIPSTITCH
is used to join two or more pieces together.

EMBROIDERY STITCHES

BACKSTITCH
is usually used as an embroidery stitch to outline or add detail. Stitches can be any length and go in any direction.

CROSS
can be used as a needle-point stitch or as an embroidery stitch stitched over background stitches with contrasting yarn or floss.

FRENCH KNOT
is usually used as an embroidery stitch to add detail. Can be made in one hole or over a bar. If dot on graph is in hole, come up and go down with needle in same hole. If dot is across a bar or over grid, come up in one hole and go down one hole over.

LAZY DAISY
is usually used as an embroidery stitch to add detail. Can be any length and go in any direction. Come up and go down in same hole, leaving loop. Come up in another hole for top of stitch, put needle through loop and go down in same hole.

STRAIGHT
is usually used as an embroidery stitch to add detail. Stitches can be any length and can go in any direction. Looks like Backstitch except stitches do not touch.

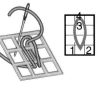

~Acknowledgments~

We would like to express our appreciation to the many people who helped create this book. Our special thanks go to each of the talented designers who contributed original designs.

We also wish to express our gratitude to the following manufacturers for their generous contribution of materials and supplies for some of the featured projects:

ALEENE'S®
All-Purpose Glue Sticks: Toy Shop Santas, Harvest Scarecrow, Dog-Gone Treats, Sweetheart Basket, Leave A Note

Thick Designer Tacky Glue: Quilt Classic Trio

Ultimate Glue Gun: Harvest Scarecrow

CARON® INTERNATIONAL
Sayelle worsted yarn: Apple Orchard, Fright Fest

CREATE-A-CRAFT
Worsted yarn: Ferris Wheel Planter

DARICE®
Canvas and canvas shapes: Toy Shop Santas, Patchwork Desk Trio, Quilt Classic Trio, Apple Orchard, Yuletide Decor, Glad Tidings, Harvest Scarecrow, Dog-Gone Treats, Barn Tissue Cover, Funny Farm Coasters, Kitchen Chickens, Farm Boy Doorstop, Swimming in the Rain, Place Mat, Christmas Door Stop, Summertime Clutch, Thank You Sampler, Teapot Coasters, Ladybug Cover, Inchworm Bag, Floral Motif, Sweetheart Basket, Mother's Helpers, Sisters Are Forever, Swan Tissue Cover, Blue Lighthouse, Leave A Note

Metallic cord: Poinsettia Coaster Set

Nylon Plus™ yarn: Patchwork Desk Trio, Summertime Clutch

Jingle bells: Star Santa

Raffia straw satin: Harvest Scarecrow

DMC®
Rayon floss: Twilight Pals

Cotton embroidery floss: Twilight Pals, Ferris Wheel Planter

Perle coton: Star Santa, Glad Tidings, Kitchen Chickens, Farm Boy Doorstop, Swimming in the Rain, Place Mat, Christmas Door Stop, Thank You Sampler, Teapot Coasters, Ladybug Cover, Summertime Clutch, Inchworm Bag, Floral Motif, Sisters Are Forever, Swan Tissue Cover

ELMER'S
Craft Bond™ Tacky Glue: Sparkling Snowflakes

J.&P. COATS / COATS & CLARK / ANCHOR
Plastic canvas yarn: Winter Warmers

Metallic blending filament: Twilight Pals

Red Heart worsted yarn: Quilt Classic Trio, Apple Orchard, Harvest Scarecrow, Sweetheart Basket

KREINIK
Metallic braid and metallic ribbon: Sparkling Snowflakes

OFFRAY
Satin ribbon: Name Card Holders

RAINBOW GALLERY®
PC7 metallic yarn: Sweetheart Basket

SANFORD
Gold coat metallic marker: Name Card Holders

UNIEK® CRAFTS

Canvas and canvas shapes: Sparkling Snow-flakes, Bell Pull, Name Card Holders

Needloft® yarn: Toy Shop Santas, Classy Cuts, Ferris Wheel Planter, Quilt Classic Trio, Bell Pull, Yuletide Decor, Star Santa, Glad Tidings, Dog-Gone Treats, Barn Tissue Cover, Funny Farm Coasters, Kitchen Chickens, Farm Boy Doorstop, Swimming in the Rain, Rainbow Mobile, Place Mat, Christmas Door Stop, Thank You Sampler, Teapot Coasters, Ladybug Cover, Inchworm Bag, Floral Motif, Bathroom Gift Set, Poinsettia Coaster Set, Mother's Helpers, Sisters Are Forever, Swan Tissue Cover, Leave A Note

Metallic cord: Sparkling Snowflakes, Classy Cuts

WESTRIM CRAFTS

Memories Are Forever Punch: Name Card Holders

WRIGHTS®

Satin ribbon: Bathroom Gift Set

YARN TREE DESIGNS

14-count metallic gold perforated paper: Sparkling Snowflakes

~Pattern Index~

~Designer Index~